ENCOURAGEMENT IN THE WILDERNESS

A Daily Devotional for Days of Discouragement, Depression, and Despair

BY

Elsie H. Brunk

ENCOURAGEMENT IN THE WILDERNESS

A Daily Devotional for Days of Discouragement, Depression, and Despair
(Previously released in ebook as: Streams of Living Water for a Thirsty Soul

By Elsie H. Brunk

Published by: Lighthouse Publishing of the Carolinas

www.lighthousepublishingofthecarolinas.com
978-1-946016-06-5

ENCOURAGEMENT IN THE WILDERNESS
A Daily Devotional for Days of Discouragement, Depression, and Despair

Unless otherwise indicated, all Scripture references are from the Holy Bible: King James Version

Scripture quotations marked (NRSV) are from the New Revised Standard Version Bible, copyright 1989, Division of Christian Education of the National Council of the Churches of Christ in the United States of America. Used by permission. All rights reserved.

Scripture quotations marked (NIV) are from the Holy Bible, New International Version.

Copyright 1973, 1978, 1984 by International Bible Society. Used by permission of Zondervan Publishing House. All rights reserved.

Table of Contents

Dedication

Dedicated to our great and awesome God—
the One whose Word inspired the writing of this book.

Acknowledgments

My deepest thanks to all of you (you know who you are) for your help, advice, and encouragement—and especially for your prayers. May God bless you richly!

Preface

*M*any years ago, God's chosen people, the Children of Israel, wandered in the wilderness for forty years. *We*, too, are God's chosen people when we accept Jesus as our Savior. But sometimes, like the Children of Israel, we find ourselves wandering in the wilderness.

I, myself, am no stranger to the wilderness. I've been there—the first time when I was seventeen years old. And I've walked alongside other weary travelers who were ready to give up along the way.

The wilderness journey can be long and lonely. But I've found, as the Children of Israel did, God is with us and cares for us in the wilderness just as He promised He would be with us *always*.

The truths and promises in ENCOURAGEMENT in the WILDERNESS have helped sustain me in my wilderness times. I pray these devotionals will help you sense God with *you* in *your* wilderness experience, and will encourage you and aid in your exit from the wilderness.

Elsie H. Brunk

A WAY IN THE WILDERNESS

"I AM ABOUT TO DO A NEW THING;
NOW IT SPRINGS FORTH, DO YOU NOT
PERCEIVE IT?
I WILL MAKE *A WAY IN THE WILDERNESS*
AND RIVERS IN THE DESERT."
ISAIAH 43:19 (NRSV)

The Wilderness

"*H*e found [Jacob] in a desert land, and in the waste howling wilderness; he led him about, he instructed him, he kept him as the apple of his eye." Deuteronomy 32:10

The wilderness! That terrible, unsettling, and sometimes terrifying desert place in our lives.

In the wilderness, we experience insecurity, loneliness, pain, and despair. Other people can sympathize and empathize and even walk with us, but no one else can carry for us the feelings that accompany our wilderness journey. Yet, good things can happen in the wilderness.

In the wilderness the Children of Israel experienced times of God's greatest activity with them. God met the Apostle Paul in the wilderness and made him into a strong missionary. In the wilderness God gave John the Baptist a sense of identity and purpose so he could tell others to prepare the way of the Lord (Matthew 3:1-3). Jesus overcame the temptations of Satan in the wilderness (Matthew 4:1-11).

It is in the wilderness that we discover who we really are—and who God is. God is with us and wants us to recognize His presence. He wants to be our light in the darkness (Psalm 112:4) and to guide us as He did the Children of Israel (Psalm 32:8). He wants to lead us about, keep us, and instruct us in the "waste howling wilderness" as He did Jacob. He wants us to learn to trust Him, learn to depend fully on Him, and to wait for His deliverance. He wants us to experience His peace as we keep our minds on Him (Isaiah 26:3). Our outward circumstances may not change, but God can bring peace and joy to us in the wilderness.

PRAYER: Here I am, God. Please do your work in me.

Related verses: Psalm 32:7, 34:4, 78:52; 107:4-9; Isaiah 35:1-6, 46:4, 58:11; Luke 4:18

God Reigns

"The Lohe Lord reigneth." Psalm 99:1

Where is God? Is He in control? Can't He do something about my situation?

Does He really know what He's doing?

When we're in the wilderness, these kinds of questions plague us. We wonder if God is as powerful as the Bible says He is. We feel out of control and everything in our lives—and even in the whole world—seems to be out of control.

The Word assures us God *is* in control, just as He always has been. Daniel says wisdom and power are God's and God is the one who changes the times and the seasons. He removes kings and sets up kings. He gives wisdom and knowledge. Daniel goes on to say God reveals deep and hidden things; He knows what's in the darkness, and light dwells with Him (Daniel 2:20-22). When we're in the darkness of the wilderness, God knows what's going on in our hard time.

If God knows when one little sparrow falls to the ground and He knows exactly how many hairs are on our heads (Matthew 10:29-30), surely He is in control of our lives and able to work in our situation. Jesus indicated that since God is in control, we need not fear. We are of more value than many sparrows (v. 31). No matter what hard things are happening in our lives, we can be assured God reigns!

PRAYER: Lord God, help me to believe You are in control and to put my hard situation into your hands.

Related verses: Psalm 93; Romans 8:31; Revelation 19:6

God's Message

" *...T*he Lord's message unto the people...I am with you, saith the Lord." Haggai 1:13.

God has a message for us when we're in the wilderness. He tells us He loves us with an everlasting love--a love that never quits, no matter what (Jeremiah 31:3). God loved us long before we were born--so much so that He gave His only Son to die for us (John 3:16). Nothing can separate us from God's love (Romans 8:38-39). Not only does God love us, but we're the apple of His eye (Zechariah 2:8). He has inscribed us on the palms of His hands (Isaiah 49:16).

God tells us He forgives our sins (I John 1:9), blots them out, and remembers them no more (Isaiah 43:25). He removes our sins from us as far as the east is from the west (Psalm 103:12).

God tells us He will never leave or forsake us (Hebrews 13:5). He promises (through Jesus) to be with us always (Matthew 28:20).

God's message gives comfort and reassurance in the wilderness.

PRAYER: Thank You, God, that I can depend on Your love, Your forgiveness, and Your presence right now in my need.

Related verses: Psalm 139:1-18; Isaiah 49:15-16

Afraid

"What time I am afraid, I will trust in [God]." Psalm 56:3

Being afraid is a normal reaction when we're in the wilderness. The unknown is scary, and even the *known* is sometimes scary. We don't know what to expect. We're afraid to face the next hour and afraid of what tomorrow will bring. We're afraid our situation will never change and we'll never feel better.

The Psalmist had times of being afraid also. But he decided at those times, the best thing he could do was to trust God. In fact, he trusted God to the extent that in his time of trouble he expected God to hide him in His pavilion and in the secret of His tabernacle (Psalm 27:5-6). He said God would set him upon a rock and his head would be lifted up above his enemies. He was so certain God would do all of those things for him that he offered up sacrifices of joy and sang praises unto the Lord.

When we're afraid, the best thing we, too, can do is trust in God. In our trouble, can *we* picture God hiding *us* as the Psalmist expected God to hide him? Can we look to God to place us on "solid ground" in our thinking so we can rise above our enemies of fear, worry, doubt, and whatever else that keeps us afraid? Can we choose to believe God is going to do this for us and therefore, joy in Him and sing praises to Him? It may have to be a sacrifice on our part to do that ahead of time, but it was a sacrifice for the Psalmist also.

PRAYER: Lord God, I am afraid, but I choose to trust You. I believe You're going to take away my doubts, fears, and worries. Please give me peace in this hard situation. I praise You, my God!

Related verses: Psalm 27:1, 112:7; Isaiah 12:2; John 14:27

Jesus Understands

"For we have not an high priest which cannot be touched with the feeling of our infirmities; but was in all points tempted like as we are, yet without sin." Hebrews 4:15

Who would understand our helpless feelings and the agony we're going through in the wilderness? Those who are most likely to understand are those who have gone through the wilderness themselves. They can offer sympathy and empathy. But even at best, their understanding and the help they can give is limited.

There is One, however, who understands us perfectly and whose help is perfect. That One is Jesus. Jesus understands our feelings of sorrow, hurt, and grief (Isaiah 53:3). He understands feelings of being let down by a person He loved (Matthew 26:69-75). Jesus understands our sadness because He felt sad and wept (John 11:35). Jesus understands our temptations and is able to help us when we're tempted (Hebrews 2:18). He experienced the feelings of facing hard times and cried to God (Matthew 26:39, 42; Hebrews 5:7). Jesus understands the feelings of being forsaken by close friends (Matthew 26:56) and even forsaken by God (Matthew 27:46). Jesus hurt physically (John 19:1, 2) and mentally (Matthew 26:38). He understands feelings of shame (Hebrews 12:2). Jesus experienced the feelings of facing death (Matthew 27:26).

Jesus not only experienced all of our feelings Himself, He also took *our* infirmities and bare *our* sicknesses (Matthew 8:16-17).

Whatever we are experiencing and feeling in the wilderness, we can rest assured Jesus knows and understands. And He can give us the help we need—anytime, anywhere.

PRAYER: Jesus, I'm so glad you know and understand what I'm going through. Please help me now!

Related verses: Job 23:10; Isaiah 63:9; Hebrews 13:12; 1 Peter 2:21, 3:18, 4:1

Choose To Believe

" *H*e that cometh to God must believe that he is, and that he is a rewarder of them that diligently seek him." Hebrews 11:6

When we're in the wilderness, it's easy to fall prey to what our feelings tell us: we'll never feel better; our situation is hopeless; God doesn't really love us; He isn't helping us solve our problems.

When we're feeling "normal," there's no struggle to believe positively in these areas. We have never seen Jesus, yet we love Him. Although we don't see Him, we believe in Him (1 Peter 1:8). That's faith—the kind we have when we feel "up." But when we're feeling "down," it's hard to have that kind of faith.

In these low times, it's important that we *choose* to believe. We have to exercise the same kind of faith when we're in the wilderness that we do when we're on the mountaintop. The difference in the wilderness is that we have to *will* to believe. Hebrews 11:1 says "faith is the substance of things hoped for, the evidence of things not seen." That's the kind of faith we need when we're in the wilderness and "don't know where we're going." When we can hardly hope to feel better and can't see anything good happening in our lives, we have to *choose* to believe God will keep His Word to us when He says, "I am with you always" (Matthew 28:20, NRSV), and when He says all things (including this wilderness experience) work together for our good (Romans 8:28).

PRAYER: O God, my feelings say one thing and Your Word says another. Help me to have the faith to believe Your Word.

Related verses: Mark 9:23-24; Romans 15:13; 2 Corinthians 5:7; Galatians 5:22

God's Kindness

"*F*or the mountains shall depart, and the hills be removed; but my kindness shall not depart from thee…saith the Lord that hath mercy on thee." Isaiah 54:10

In Isaiah 54:10, God is promising His continued kindness and peace almost immediately after He tells us, "for a small moment have I forsaken thee" and "in a little wrath I hid my face from thee for a moment" (Isaiah 54:7-8).

In the wilderness we feel as though God has forsaken us and has hidden His face from us. But God goes on to say: "but with great mercies will I gather thee" and "with everlasting kindness will I have mercy on thee" (v.8). For whatever reason God is "forsaking" us and "hiding His face" from us, He is promising us it's only for a short time and then He will again work in our behalf. In verse 10, He promises His kindness will always be with us.

The words in verse 11 describe our wilderness state: "afflicted, tossed with tempest, and not comforted." But God has a further promise for us: "I will lay thy stones with fair colours, and lay thy foundations with sapphires."

These verses reaffirm that God still has us in mind when we're feeling low and can't sense His presence. They also reaffirm that God will bring us out of the wilderness.

PRAYER: Lord God, thank You for Your promise that Your kindness will never depart from me. Thank You, too, for the reassurances that You will bring me out of the wilderness.

Related verses: Deuteronomy 4:31; Psalm 117; 119:76; Ephesians 2:4-7

GOD WITH US

"*I*t is the Lord who goes before you. He will be with you; he will not fail you or forsake you. Do not fear or be dismayed." Deuteronomy 31:8 (NRSV)

What in your life right now do you find difficult to face? Do you wish you didn't have to get up in the morning and face another day? Has life lost meaning? Do you lack direction? Perhaps you are fearful because of things you have to do or places you have to go.

When Moses turned over the leadership of the Children of Israel to Joshua, he gave Joshua some wise and encouraging words from God. Moses knew how overwhelmed Joshua must feel because he, himself, had felt incapable and overwhelmed forty years earlier when God had called him to lead the Children of Israel. Moses told Joshua it was the Lord who would lead the way and who would be with him and not fail or forsake him. He also told Joshua to "fear not, neither be dismayed."

Moses' words of encouragement are for you in the wilderness. Whether you simply need to be faithful in living through each day—or God is calling you to some special task—rest assured God will be with you and go before you as He went before Joshua and the Children of Israel (Exodus 13:21). God will lead you. He won't fail or forsake you. He says to you, "Fear not, nor be dismayed."

PRAYER: Lord God, Your words are my hope as I seek to follow You. Knowing You are with me each day and won't fail or forsake me, gives me courage to face the wilderness and the tasks to which you have called me.

Related verses: Exodus 33:14; Deuteronomy 2:7; Joshua 1:9; Psalm 73:23; Hebrews 13:5

DARKNESS

"Who is among you that feareth the Lord, that obeyeth the voice of his servant, that walketh in darkness, and hath no light? Let [them] trust in the name of the Lord, and stay upon [their] God." Isaiah 50:10

According to Isaiah, even though we are Christians we can experience dark times in our lives. The darkness mentioned here is not the darkness of evil which the New Testament refers to (Matthew 6:23), but rather the darkness—or wilderness experience—that trials and hard times can bring.

Some of us know about the "dark night of the soul." We feel overwhelmed. We feel as though we're in the depths. It seems we can go no lower. There's nothing but blackness.

But Isaiah says the way out of the darkness is to "trust in the name of the Lord, and stay (rely) upon God." The word "stay" denotes a reliance on or belief in God that says, "I know that I know that I know God is who He says He is and He will do what He says He will do. No matter what, I will trust Him." To stay upon God means to cling to Him, lean hard on Him, and to wait patiently for His deliverance.

Sometimes it takes a long time to get through the darkness. We can get weary in the process and think, *What's the use?* But if we keep going and stay (rely) on God, He will bring us to the light.

PRAYER: Deliverer God, in my dark time, help me to trust You and to lean upon You and cling to You, waiting patiently for Your light.

Related verses: 2 Samuel 22:29; Psalm 18:28, 107:13-14, 112:4, 139:11-12; Isaiah 9:2; Daniel 2:22; Micah 7:8

COMPLETE WORK

"... *He* which hath begun a good work in you will perform it until the day of Jesus Christ." Philippians 1:6

When we're in the wilderness, we sometimes feel our life is useless. It seems like we're "off the track." We think, *What's life all about anyway? Why am I even here?*

But if we're trusting God with our lives, we can rest assured He knows what's going on with us. He made us and understands exactly what's happening in our bodies, minds, and spirits. He began "a good work" in us and even though we aren't where we'd like to be mentally and emotionally right now, we are assured in Philippians 1:6 that God will keep on completing the good work He started.

God will use this suffering we're going through as part of His work to bring us into our place as "heirs and joint-heirs with Christ" (Romans 8:17). We're told in Revelation 21:7 that if we overcome, we will inherit all things. And there is laid up for us a crown of righteousness which the Lord will give us (2 Timothy 4:8).

So take heart in the fact that a loving God who has such wonderful things planned for you, His child, will keep working in your life day by day to complete the work He has begun in you. And He is doing that right now—even while you're in the wilderness.

PRAYER: Lord God, thank You that I can trust You to complete the good work You started in me. Help me to be patient during the process.

Related verses: Jeremiah 29:11; Romans 8:14-18

LOOKING UNTO JESUS

"... *Let* us lay aside every weight, and the sin which doth so easily beset us, and let us run with patience the race that is set before us, looking unto Jesus the author and finisher of our faith." Hebrews 12:1-2

What is it that is like a weight in my life—in yours? What causes us to go into the wilderness? Perhaps it's a bad habit that keeps us from experiencing abundant life and health. Or an unforgiving spirit. Is there an area of intemperance such as excessive eating, overworking, or overspending? Is there a problem with self-indulgence? All of these can be weights in our lives. We are told to lay aside every weight.

What sin tends to trip me up the quickest? Is it lust, greed, ungratefulness, resentment, worry, or bitterness? I am to lay that sin aside also.

The days, weeks, and months ahead are part of the race that is set before us. We are told to run the race with patience. But the course contains many rough places. It's so easy to become weary of the continual hard things that come our way. The wilderness causes us to feel like giving up—calling it quits. How can we endure and remain faithful? There's only one way, and that's "looking unto Jesus"—trusting Him to empower us for this race. Trusting Him to enable us to lay aside the weights and sins. Trusting Him to get us through—or over—everything that would keep us from completing this race for His honor and glory. Trusting Him to perfect our faith.

PRAYER: Sometimes the way becomes so hard, Lord God. I choose to look to Jesus, trusting His power as I go through the wilderness.

Related verses: Matthew 1:21; Mark 8:34-35; 1 Corinthians 9:24

RESTORATION

"… *He* leadeth me beside the still waters. He restoreth my soul." Psalm 23:2-3

After I had gone through the wilderness several times, I finally realized God has His purposes in allowing wilderness experiences in our lives. Then, instead of my usual struggle in the wilderness, I began to surrender to God and pray: *Here I am, God. When it's Your timing, bring me out of the wilderness. And please help me to learn all You want me to learn while I'm here.* Then I would "hang loose" and not weary myself with struggling and trying to make myself feel better. And I praised God and tried to be open for answers from Him and what He wanted to teach me.

Long-time missionary, Amy Carmichael, said: "God cannot speak to a restless soul any easier than you can see quiet reflections in a restless pool." Mulling over our hard situation and letting negative thoughts control our mind hinders our hearing from God. But if we quiet our thoughts and wait with trust and expectancy for God to work in us (Psalm 46:10), He will lead us beside the still waters and restore our souls. When we wait on the Lord and take courage, He will strengthen our hearts (Psalm 27:14).

PRAYER: Help me, God, to quiet my mind so I can hear what You want to say to me.

Related verses: Psalm 25:5, 37:7, 62:5-8; Proverbs 1:33; Isaiah 30:15,18, 57:18; Jeremiah 30:10

FORGIVEN

"*A*ll we like sheep have gone astray; we have all turned to our own way, and the Lord has laid on him the iniquity of us all." Isaiah 53:6 (NRSV)

God has made a way for sinners—and all Christians are sinners saved by grace. Even we redeemed sinners sometimes go astray and turn to our own way. Then we may find it hard to accept God's forgiveness and perhaps even harder yet, to forgive ourselves, especially when we're in the wilderness. But we need to remember that most of God's saints in the Bible had their times of failure.

Noah got drunk (Genesis 9:20-21). Abram told his wife, Sarai, to lie (Genesis 12:11-13). Jacob deceived his father (Genesis 27:21-24). Moses spoke without thinking (Psalm106:32-33). Joshua failed to ask God's counsel (Joshua 9:1-15). David committed adultery and had an innocent man murdered (2 Samuel 11:4,15-17). Yet in Hebrews 11:39 we're told, "these all obtained a good report through faith."

If we, who are God's people sometimes fail Him and "we confess our sins, He is faithful and just to forgive us our sins, and to cleanse us from all unrighteousness" (1 John 1:9). We have to believe that promise and accept His forgiveness.

PRAYER: Thank You, God, that You have provided a way for me to be forgiven through Jesus, who was willing to bear the sins of us all.

Related verses: Psalm 51:1-2; 130:1-5; Isaiah 43:25; Romans 5:6-9; 1 John 2:1-2

GOD'S DWELLING PLACE

"For thus saith the high and lofty One that inhabiteth eternity, whose name is Holy; I dwell in the high and holy place, with him also that is of a contrite and humble spirit, to revive the spirit of the humble, and to revive the heart of the contrite ones." Isaiah 57:15

Isn't it wonderful that our God—the high and Holy God who dwells in the high and holy place (Heaven)—is also willing, and even wants, to dwell with mere humans? There seems to be a condition, however, for God to dwell with us, and the condition is that we have a contrite and humble spirit.

Our pride in thinking we can work out our own problems can lead us into the wilderness. But sooner or later we experience contriteness and humility. We come to realize we can't change our situation nor the people in it. There is nothing we can do. We finally see we are totally dependent on God. When we get to this place and recognize *we* can't change *anything*, including ourselves and our feelings, God can work in us. He says His dwelling place is with us in our contriteness and humbleness and He will revive our spirits and our hearts. Let's take hope in that promise.

PRAYER: God, I give this situation and myself to You. There's nothing I can do. Please revive my heart and spirit.

Related verses: 2 Chronicles 34:27; Job 22:29; Psalm 34:18, 51:17; Proverbs 16:19; Isaiah 66:1-2; Matthew 5:3,5; Colossians 3:12; James 4:6

REFINED AND PURIFIED

"... *He* is like a refiner's fire and like fuller's soap; he will sit as a refiner and purifier of silver..." Malachi3:2 (NRSV)

Every spring I have to make an adjustment in my life. I have to "switch gears" from reading, writing, and pursuing projects I enjoy—to gardening, yard work, and other tasks which, for me, are pure work.

One spring it was especially hard for me to make that adjustment. In fact, I struggled with it all summer and felt terribly discouraged. I couldn't understand why I was going through the wilderness.

Then one day I read Malachi 3:2 and immediately knew there was something in it for me. The phrase "he shall sit as a refiner and purifier of silver" caught my eye. I did some research and found in those days a refiner of silver sat by the fire as the silver was being purified, watching closely that the fire didn't get too hot or too cold.

"That's what I've been doing for you all summer," God spoke to my heart. He had been watching that my struggle didn't get out of hand, but that "the fire" was just right for my refining and purifying.

How wonderful to know we're in safe hands when we go through the refining and purifying we need in order to mature as God's people.

PRAYER: Thank You, God, for keeping the "fire" just right in my refining process.

Related verses: Deuteronomy 4:20; Isaiah 48:10; Zechariah 13:9; Titus 2:13-14; 1 John 3:1-3

GOD'S PROMISES

"For in [Jesus] every one of God's promises is a 'Yes.' For this reason it is through him that we say the 'Amen,' to the glory of God." 2 Corinthians 1:20 (NRSV)

It's hard to believe and to have faith when we're going through the wilderness. Our low and desperate feelings cause our thoughts to dwell on the negative. Feelings are important and we need to face them and deal with them, but we must remember they are transient. Feelings can be changed by the weather, the actions or words of another person, and even by what we ourselves do or don't do. If we eat too much or the wrong foods, get insufficient exercise, or miss sleep, our feelings will be affected. Therefore, we can't depend on our feelings to accurately guide our thoughts.

Just the opposite is true of God's promises. They never change. They're always the same no matter what. We can depend on them. The verse in 2 Corinthians says in Jesus every one of God's promises is a "yes." That means they are true, and God through Jesus keeps every promise in His Word. Therefore, we can agree and say "Amen" (so let it be), even though our feelings say differently.

When we're feeling low, we need to focus our minds on—and persist in believing—the promises in God's Word, instead of believing only what our feelings tell us.

PRAYER: O God, help me to concentrate on and believe Your never-changing promises, rather than letting my feelings rule my thoughts and actions.

Related verses: Deuteronomy 7:9; Joshua 21:45; 2 Peter 1:3-4. Some of God's promises: Psalm 9:9, 145:19; Isaiah 41:10, 43:25, 65:24; Jeremiah 29:11, 33:3; Matthew 7:7-8; 1 John 1:9

FACTS---NOT FEELINGS

"*C*asting down imaginations, and every high thing that exalteth itself against the knowledge of God, and bringing into captivity every thought to the obedience of Christ." 2 Corinthians 10:5

When we let our low feelings determine our thinking, the resulting negative thoughts are indeed imaginations. These imaginations are not the knowledge (facts) God gives in His Word. What are some of our imaginations in light of God's facts?

Imagination: *God doesn't care about me.* Facts: We are important and precious to God. We are "the apple of his eye" (Zechariah 2:8). God chose us to be His special people (1 Peter 2:9).

Imagination: *I messed up and I'm no good. Why keep trying?* Facts: If we confess our sins, God will forgive us and cleanse us from all unrighteousness (I John 1:9). We can begin again with a clean slate.

Imagination: *I'll never get out of the wilderness.* Facts: The Lord restores our souls and leads us in right paths. He is with us and comforts us in our darkest valleys (Psalm 23:3-4). God is our God forever and ever and will be our guide even unto death (Psalm 48:14).

We need to cast down (replace) our negative thoughts (imaginations) with the facts of God's Word—facts that are true and always dependable. God wants us to surrender our negative thoughts in obedience to Him.

PRAYER: Help me, God, to dwell on facts instead of feelings. Help me to replace my imaginations with the truth of Your Word.

Related verses: Psalm 138:8; Isaiah 25:1; Psalm 73:24-26; Jeremiah 29:11

GIVE NEGATIVE TO GOD

"... *T*he Lord was my stay." Psalm 18:18

We determine in our hearts we will let go of the negative and dwell on the positive. We declare with the Psalmist: "I will yet praise him, who is the health of my countenance, and my God" (Psalm 42:11). But our feelings still don't agree with our determinations. We're still plagued with negative thoughts and the battle to let go of them is hard. What can we do?

When we give our negative thoughts to God and they come back, we have to *immediately* give them to God *again*, and then turn our thoughts to something positive. If the thoughts come back two minutes later, we have to give them to God again—immediately! And again turn our thoughts to something positive. If the thoughts come back fifteen minutes later, we have to repeat the process—and *keep on repeating the process every time negative thoughts come back into our mind.* The important thing is to *immediately* turn them over to God—not entertain them in our minds awhile first and then decide to give them to God.

We have to "stand fast in the Lord" (Philippians 4:1) against negative thoughts. He is our rock, our fortress, our deliverer, our strength, our buckler, the horn of our salvation, and our high tower (Psalm 18:2). "I will call upon the Lord, who is worthy to be praised: so shall I be saved from mine enemies [negative thoughts]" (v. 3). Continually giving negative thoughts to God and then concentrating on praising Him is the best way to restore our trust in Him. He is our stay (Psalm 18:18).

PRAYER: Help me, God, to apply Your discipline to overcome these negative thoughts. Please remind me to *immediately* give them to you and to turn my mind to the positive and to praising You. Thank You, my Deliverer.

Related verses: Deuteronomy 33:27; Psalm 34:7; Isaiah 12:6; Psalm 18:31-33

CHRIST'S STRENGTH

"*I* can do all things through Christ which strengtheneth me." Philippians 4:13

Our hard situations seem impossible when we're in the wilderness.

What are you facing today? Is it something difficult? Something scary? Something you know God wants you to do but you'd rather *not* do? Something you feel you can't do in your own strength? Perhaps it's a physical problem and you must go through a painful medical procedure to correct it. Or maybe you are involved in a hurtful relationship and need to choose a positive and loving reaction toward the other person. Is it that someone you love is making unwise and ungodly choices and all you can do is trust them to God for His keeping and changing? Are you in a situation in which God wants you to "hang in there" but you're tempted to take the easy way and "cop out"? Are you finding it hard to believe the facts of God's Word and His promises instead of letting your feelings determine your thinking? Are you afraid to take steps out of the darkness of the wilderness?

The words of Philippians 4:13 are for you today. You can claim Christ's strength for "all things" He wants you to do.

PRAYER: Lord Jesus, give me faith to believe that with Your strength I can do whatever You want me to do today.

Related verses: Isaiah 40:29-31; Matthew 6:34; Mark 13:11; 2 Corinthians 12:9-10

THE FAITH WALK

"... *W*e walk by faith, not by sight." 2 Corinthians 5:7

The Christian life is a walk of faith from beginning to end. We didn't have the privilege of seeing (with our physical eyes) the risen Jesus before we believed and accepted Him, as Thomas did (John 20:24-28). Thomas' belief in Jesus came by sight. Ours comes through faith (believing without seeing). Jesus pronounced a blessing on those who have not seen and yet have believed (v. 29). As we walk with God, our testimony becomes, "We have known and believed the love God hath for us" (1 John 4:16).

Walking by faith is easy when all is going well and we're feeling close to God. Perhaps it's because we can "see" God working in our situation. And we can "feel" His love for us. Does this kind of walk really take faith?

The walk requiring faith is one of difficulties and wilderness experiences, when we can't "see" God working nor "feel" His love. We want to cry out as Jesus did, "My God, my God, why have You forsaken Me?" (Matthew 27:46, NIV). We feel as the Psalmist did when he said, "Hath God forgotten to be gracious? hath he in anger shut up his tender mercies?" (Psalm 77:9).

How do we walk by faith in hard situations? We have to set our will and determine *nothing* will move us away from our belief in God (Isaiah 50:7). We have to reaffirm our faith in God again and again (Psalm 77:10-14), reminding ourselves of His faithfulness (Psalm 89:1). We have to *choose* to believe and to trust God (Psalm 37:5).

PRAYER: Lord God, in these hard times when I can't see the way nor feel Your love for me, help me to trust You and to walk by sheer faith in You.

Related verses: Psalm 62:6, 119:89-90; Lamentations 3:22-26; Mark 9:23-24; Luke 17:5; Romans 1:17; Hebrews 11:l; 1 Peter 1:8

FOLLOW ON TO KNOW GOD

"*T*hen shall we know, if we follow on to know the Lord…"
Hosea 6:3

We all desire to know God. But how do we learn to know Him? According to Hosea, we learn to know God by keeping on following Him (doing His will) and seeking to know Him.

"Following on to know God" is hard work. It takes a long time (all our lives), and many people don't want to wait. They want quick, easy answers instead of being willing to wait for God's answers in His timing. They look for solutions that cater to their own wants and desires instead of following God's way. They try to make God into their own image instead of letting Him mold them into *His* image. In their impatience and self-will they give up following on to know God and miss learning to know Him and His ways and working in their lives.

In the wilderness we may be tempted to go our own way instead of "following on" to know God. Perhaps we're feeling God isn't answering our prayers or He isn't working in the way—or in the time frame—we expect, and we wonder if the effort to follow God is really worth it. Will we still follow on to know the Lord by staying close to God's Word in the Bible, or will we decide to seek answers elsewhere—in some other belief system such as New Age or Eastern Religions?

Maybe we're being chastened by the Lord (Hebrews 12:9-10) and we don't like it. Will we accept the chastening and "follow on to know the Lord," or will we give in to resentment and bitterness and give up seeking a deeper spiritual life from God?

PRAYER: O God, give me a deep desire to follow on to know You. Help me to put aside impatience and self-will and to wait for You in every situation in my life.

Related verses: Exodus 33:13-14; Deuteronomy 4:29-31; 2 Samuel 22:31-33; Psalm 9:10; Jeremiah 24:7; John 7:17, 10:14; 1 John 2:3-6

NOT BY WORKS

"For by grace you have been saved through faith, and this is not your own doing; it is the gift of God—not the result of works, so that no one may boast." Ephesians 2:8-9, (NRSV)

When we're in the wilderness, often our feelings aren't what we would like them to be. We may even feel we are no good to others or to God. We're barely able to carry out the necessary everyday tasks, much less able to do other significant work. This tends to make us feel guilty. We feel we should be doing the good deeds we would normally be doing if we weren't in the wilderness.

There *is* something to be said for going ahead and doing good deeds if at all possible. Doing for others is therapeutic in many ways. It takes our minds off ourselves and our problems, and gives us a better perspective. Doing for others also gives us satisfaction and self-esteem.

But if we can't continue our good deeds for awhile, we needn't feel guilty. The Bible tells us plainly we aren't saved by our good deeds. Our salvation is totally a gift from God and not of our own doing. Our salvation is purely an act of God's grace, and that means even if we feel we don't deserve it. God knows our hearts (that we would like to be doing good deeds) and He knows too, we won't be in the wilderness forever.

Perhaps a break from doing good deeds gives us a chance to hear from God in a new way. It can also remind us anew it's our acceptance of what God through Jesus has done for us that determines our salvation.

PRAYER: Thank You, God, that You understand my situation and You know my desire to be doing for others. Help me to rest in Your love and to hear what You want to say to me while I'm in the wilderness.

Related verses: Romans 4:1-7, 11:6; 2 Timothy 1:9

FROM GLORY TO GLORY

"Moses said, 'Show me your glory, I pray.'" Exodus 33:18 (NRSV)

When Moses asked God to see God's glory, God told him He could not show Moses His face. John 1:14-18 says no one has ever seen God; He is made known by His Son, Jesus, and we see the glory of God in the glory of Jesus. Furthermore, in 2 Corinthians 3:18 we find we're reflections of the glory of the Lord and we're being changed into His likeness from glory to glory by the Holy Spirit.

In the marginal notes of one Bible, it says "from glory to glory" denotes character change. That means the Holy Spirit is doing a work in our character to change us into the likeness of God. Although that work is being done in us *now*, we won't have God's perfect likeness until we get to Heaven.

When we're in the wilderness, we sometimes feel it will take a long time for the Holy Spirit to "change us from glory to glory into God's likeness." We feel we're slow learners. We learn a spiritual lesson, then find we have to learn it all over again later. But it gives us hope to know we're not expected to learn everything all at once. We're changed by degrees (from glory to glory). And perhaps it's not that we have to learn the exact same lesson over, but another aspect or a deeper truth. God knows exactly what is needed in our spiritual development and we can trust Him to bring that about.

PRAYER: Thank You, God, that when we open our lives to the Holy Spirit, He makes the necessary character changes to bring us into Your glory.

Related verses: Romans 6:4-6; 2 Corinthians 4:6; Colossians 3:10; Psalm 27:8

LIKE TREES

"But I am like a green olive tree in the house of God: I trust in the mercy of God forever and ever." Psalm 52:8

God's people (Christians) are often likened to trees in the Old Testament. Jeremiah 17:7-8 (NRSV) says blessed are those who trust in the Lord and whose trust is the Lord. They will be like trees planted by water. They won't be afraid when heat comes, but will stay green, and when drought comes, they won't be anxious and they will always bear fruit.

When we picture a tree by the water, we see a strong, healthy tree—one that withstands all kinds of outer forces and pressures. It bends and sways when the winds and weather beat upon it, but it remains upright and full of life.

We can be like that tree. As we take God's Word and the Holy Spirit into our "roots," we become spiritually and emotionally strong so when the forces and pressures of life (even the wilderness) bombard us, we will be flexible and stay emotionally and spiritually healthy and full of life. We won't fear when "heat" (hard times) come. When "drought" (dry times) come, we won't be anxious. We will keep on bearing Spirit fruit in our service for God.

PRAYER: Lord God, fill me with Yourself that I may trust You and be like the tree planted by the water.

Related verses: Psalm 1:1-3, 92:12-14

DELIGHTING IN GOD'S WILL

"*I* delight to do your will, O my God; your law is within my heart." Psalm 40:8 (NRSV)

There are times in our lives when we struggle with "delighting" to do the will of God. We know the way the Lord wants us to go and how He wants us to react in certain situations, and we desire to obey Him. But it isn't easy.

Self in us wants to have its way and we have to die to self in order to follow God's will. The struggle of dying to self is painful, and that pain prevents us from experiencing an immediate delight in obeying God. In order to delight to do God's will, His law has to be "in our hearts"—that means the desire to obey God's law. Many people have God's law in their heads (they know God's law), but the desire to obey is not in their hearts.

When we're younger, we sometimes have yet to experience the depths of peace, joy, and satisfaction that come with dying to self and doing God's will. As we get older and have known those blessings, we find it easier to say with the Psalmist, "I delight to do Your will, O my God!"

PRAYER: Thank You, God that You bring us to the place of delighting to do Your will. Thank You, too, for your blessings of peace, joy, and satisfaction when we obey You.

Related verses: Psalm 1:2, 25:10, 37:31, 143:10; Jeremiah 31:33; Romans 7:22, 12:1-2; Hebrews 5:8

INNER STRENGTH

"*My* flesh and my heart faileth: but God is the strength of my heart, and my portion for ever." Psalm 73:26

One of the blessings of our oldest daughter's marriage to her now-husband, Jon, was the friendship I enjoyed with Jon's mother.

Helen and I found we were kindred spirits in our love for the Lord. When she and her husband, Bob, came from Ohio to visit their family, Helen and I always enjoyed getting together and sharing what God was doing in our lives.

A number of years ago, Helen was diagnosed with cancer. During the years between that time and her death, Helen and Bob came to see their family regularly. She had many surgeries, but when she felt better they would come once again. I knew she was probably in pain and it must have been awfully hard for her to travel, but Helen depended on God for her strength and always had a vibrant testimony for Him, even when her physical body was failing. God was indeed the strength of Helen's heart and her portion forever. Then, as she was dying she whispered, "It's beautiful!" God was no doubt giving her a glimpse of Heaven.

What an example of courage and faith for us in the wilderness. We, too, can have God as "the strength of [our hearts] and [our] portion forever."

PRAYER: Help me, Lord God, to find You as the strength of my heart right now in the wilderness. I want You to be my portion forever.

Related verses: Psalm 16:5, 18:2, 27:1, 28:7, 29:11, 46:1; Isaiah 12:2, 26:4

MANY TEMPTATIONS

"... *Though* now for a season, if need be, ye are in heaviness through [many] temptations." I Peter 1:6

Does it seem to you Satan's temptations come in bunches? For awhile he'll let us alone. And then suddenly, he's after us again and seems to hound us relentlessly for awhile. He knows our weaknesses and the areas that trip us up the quickest, and that's where he deals his hardest and longest attacks. He seems to think if he keeps at it long enough, he'll wear us down and gain the victory. He would like nothing better than to drive us into the wilderness. And sometimes he does!

In James 4:7-8 (NRSV), we're given the strategy for getting rid of Satan. "Submit yourselves therefore to God. Resist the devil, and he will flee from you. Draw near to God, and he will draw near to you."

We are not to try to be strong in ourselves, but in the power of God's might and to use the armor He provides for us (Ephesians 6:10-18).

When Satan sees we mean business in overcoming his temptations, he will let us alone—at least for awhile. We have to start resisting him *immediately* though, because the longer we let his ideas and suggestions stay in our minds, the longer and harder will be the battle to get rid of him.

PRAYER: Help me, God, to remember to start resisting Satan *immediately* when his temptations come. Thank You for providing the way for me to have victory over him.

Related verses: Luke 11:4, 22:31-32; 1 Corinthians 10:13; 2 Corinthians 11:3,14,15; Ephesians 4:27; Hebrews 2:18, 4:14-16; James 1:12; 1 Peter 5:8-9

OUR CROSS

"And [Jesus] bearing his cross went forth into a place called...Golgotha: where they crucified Him." John 19:17-18

How much more could Jesus endure? He had been criticized, rejected, let down by His closest friends, denied by one of His chosen disciples and betrayed by another, slapped, spit on, mocked, whipped, given an unfair trial, and condemned to die. As if all that weren't enough, He was now required to carry His own cross. His poor body, wracked with pain, must have protested with the little energy left in it. And He must have wanted to shout, "No way! No more!" But He didn't.

He took up that heavy cross and tried to carry it. He did it for me—for you—for everyone. He took upon Himself all the sins of the world. And He died!

Jesus is our Hero—the only One worth following. And in order to be His followers, we must deny ourselves and take up our cross (the hard things in our lives) and follow Him (Matthew 16:24). Will we accept our suffering in the wilderness as being a part of His suffering (1 Peter 4:12-13)? Will we determine to walk through the wilderness for His honor and glory? Will we believe in Him, no matter what?

Jesus went all the way for us. Will we do the same for Him?

PRAYER: Lord Jesus, thank You for going all the way to the cross and dying for me. Help me to be willing to bear my cross and follow You.

Related verses: Romans 5:6-8, 8:33-34; 1 Corinthians 15:3-4; 2 Corinthians 5:15; 1 Thessalonians 5:9-10; Isaiah 53:3-6

GOD—OUR HOPE

"... *T*hou art my hope in the day of evil." Jeremiah 17:17

We are truly living in evil days. With the reports we read in the newspapers and hear on radio and TV, we wonder how the world can get much worse. It seems no one is safe anywhere anymore, and fear threatens to take hold of us.

Jeremiah's words, "The heart is deceitful above all things and desperately wicked" (17:9), seem all the more true of today and we sometimes are tempted to despair and wonder if it's worth the effort that is put into programs to help people improve.

When we're in the wilderness, these feelings of hopelessness are sometimes magnified. The needs we see become overwhelming.

The world situation must have been that way back in Jeremiah's day too. How was Jeremiah able to see God as His hope in a hard situation? Because he trusted God. Trust is the *action* part of hope and hope is the *feeling* part of trust. When we trust, we hope. When we hope, we trust.

PRAYER: Lord God, help me not to despair when I see the evil around me, but to focus on You and put my hope in You.

Related verses: Psalm 31:24, 71:1-5, 112:7, 121:7, Jeremiah 17:7-8; Lamentations 3:26

WHERE IS GOD?

"*O* Lord,...thou didst hide thy face, and I was troubled. I cried to thee, O Lord; and unto the Lord I made supplication." Psalm 30:7-8

The Psalmist went through wilderness experiences in which he felt God was hiding His face from him (see also Psalm 10:1 and chapter 13).

When we're in the wilderness, often we too, feel God is hiding His face from us. When we pray, our prayers seem to go no higher than the ceiling, and sometimes we are tempted to quit praying altogether.

There is, however, a more helpful way to respond when wilderness times come and God seems to be hiding His face. We can start by telling God, "I don't sense Your presence and my prayers seem to be going nowhere, but I'm going to talk to You anyway." Then we can proceed to talk to God as though He were right with us and to tell Him whatever is on our minds. And it really helps!

We don't have to *feel* God's presence in order to talk to Him. He promises in Hebrews 13:5 He will never leave or forsake us. He *is* with us, whether or not we feel His presence.

PRAYER: God, in my wilderness times when I can't sense Your presence, help me to accept by faith that You are with me. And help me to keep talking to You.

Related verses: 2 Samuel 22:7; Psalm 27:5-10, 31:22, 102:1-2; Isaiah 54:7-8

HOMESCHOOLED BY GOD

"The Lord giveth wisdom: out of his mouth cometh knowledge and understanding." Proverbs 2:6

What knowledge is available today! Because of knowledge, people have been to the moon and back. Because of knowledge we enjoy the benefits of cars, computers, and microwaves.

Many people have had the opportunity of furthering their education and getting degrees. Then there are those people who haven't had that opportunity. And because they haven't, some people struggle with feelings of inferiority and low self-esteem and even succumb to the wilderness.

But Proverbs 2:6 says it is the Lord who gives wisdom and from Him comes knowledge and understanding. All of us have the opportunity of learning from God. We can study His Word, seek to abide in Jesus, and open our lives to the Holy Spirit who is the greatest Teacher (John 14:26).

God can give wisdom, knowledge, and understanding far beyond that which is learned from books. There is no need for those who don't have degrees to feel inferior if they are open to learning from God. Being "home-schooled" by God provides the best of education.

PRAYER: Lord God, I want Your kind of wisdom, knowledge, and understanding. Teach me by Your precious Holy Spirit.

Related verses: Psalm 25:9, 119:130; Luke 4:22, 21:15; 1 Corinthians 1:25-31; James 1:5

SINGLE EYE

"The light of the body is the eye: if therefore thine eye be single, thy whole body shall be full of light." Matthew 6:22

I've often wondered just what Matthew 6:22 means. Does it mean if our single purpose in life is to follow God, then we'll have light for our way? Perhaps so. But there are certain situations in my life when I think of this verse.

At those times when there are so many tasks to be done or so many events to get through, when life seems too busy or too full, it helps me to have a "single eye" (especially if I'm in the wilderness). If I just concentrate on one thing at a time, focus in on it, and trust God to help me get it done, instead of continually looking at the *whole* picture and worrying about how I'm going to get through all the events, I don't get the feeling of being overwhelmed as quickly. Discouragement can easily settle in when a person looks at the whole picture or at the whole immediate future. If we take one day at a time—or better yet, one hour or one minute at a time, trusting the Lord for help—life doesn't seem so impossible.

PRAYER: Lord God, help me to have a single eye both to serve You and in facing what life brings my way.

Related verses: Psalm 25:5, 33:20, 46:1, 59:16, 63:7, 121:1-2, 138:3; Isaiah 41:10, 13, 50:7; Matthew 6:34; Hebrews 4:14-16

JESUS WITH US

"*L*o, I am with you alway, even unto the end of the world." Matthew 28:20

Before Jesus left this earth and went to heaven, He commissioned His disciples to carry on His work. He also promised them He would be with them always.

Jesus' commission and promise are for His followers today also. How wonderful to know Jesus is always with us. We don't have to struggle to carry on His work by ourselves. We don't have to feel like it all depends entirely on us. He wants to help and empower us. We don't have to feel lonely, because Jesus is with us as our Companion and Guide. He will walk with us day by day, moment by moment. Jesus is with us in our hard times and wilderness experiences even though we don't always feel His presence. But we have to believe His presence is with us in order for Him to be—and do—all He wants to be and do for us. Jesus promises, "I will never leave thee, nor forsake thee" (Hebrews 13:5).

PRAYER: Lord Jesus, thank You for Your presence with me always. Help me to let You be all You want to be and do for me.

Related verses: Deuteronomy 31:6,8; Isaiah 41:10; Psalm 139:7-12; Hebrews 13:5

GOD'S GUIDANCE

"*I* will instruct thee and teach thee in the way which thou shalt go: I will guide thee with mine eye." Psalm 32:8

It's lonely in the wilderness—and scary. The way is long and hard, and we don't know which way to turn—or who to turn to. We feel weak and vulnerable. And sometimes we feel as though we're the only ones going through the wilderness. We may even fear certain people and what they may do to us.

But even though we feel forsaken by others—and perhaps even by God, *God is with us right where we are.* He wants us to turn to Him and know Him as our light and salvation, so we won't have to be afraid of others (Psalm 27:1). He wants to be our helper so we can boldly say, "I will not fear what [others] shall do unto me" (Hebrews 13:6).

God wants to be our strength and our shield. He wants us to trust in Him and be helped so we can rejoice and praise Him (Psalm 28:7). God wants to be our rock, our fortress, our deliverer, our refuge, high tower, and savior (2 Samuel 22:2-3). God wants to be our defense (Psalm 62:2,6) so that when the enemy (Satan) comes in like a flood, the Spirit of the Lord will lift up a standard against him (Isaiah 59:19).

We are not alone in the wilderness. God is with us and He wants us to trust Him to lead and guide us.

PRAYER: O God, thank You for assuring me in Your Word You're with me in this wilderness. I trust You to lead and guide me.

Related verses: Psalm 31:3, 63:1-8; Isaiah 58:11; John 16:13

DISAPPOINTMENTS

"… *P*erfect through sufferings." Hebrews 2:10

Disappointments! Disappointments!

Sometimes it seems as though life is nothing but disappointments, one after the other. We work through each one, and for awhile are free of the affects of our disappointment. Then along comes another, and all the past disappointments come back to hound us too. Too many disappointments can send us into the wilderness.

Why is life so full of disappointments? We don't know. But God can use our disappointments to perfect us. Hebrews 2:10 tells us even Jesus was made perfect through suffering. He went through disappointments, sorrow, and grief too. He was despised and rejected (Isaiah 53:3).

Perhaps we feel no one understands our disappointments. The Psalmist felt that way when he said, "Reproach hath broken my heart; and I am full of heaviness: and I looked for some to take pity, but there was none; and for comforters, but I found none" (Psalm 69:20).

If no one else understands our disappointments, we know Jesus does. We can go to Him and tell Him how we're feeling and seek His comfort and strength in our disappointments.

PRAYER: Thank You, Jesus, that You're there for me when no one else understands. I need your comfort and strength.

Related verses: Psalm 116:3, 142:4; Matthew 26:38-39; Luke 22:44

IS GOD ENOUGH?

"... *T*o humble thee, and to prove thee, to know what was in thine heart, whether thou wouldest keep his commandments, or no." Deuteronomy 8:2

God said He led the Children of Israel in the wilderness for 40 years to see what was in their hearts and whether or not they would obey him.

What do the hard times—the wilderness experiences—in our lives mean? Could it be that God allows them in order to see if we will continue to follow Him? To see if *He* is enough in our lives? When it seems all of life is out of control, when all our "props" are removed, what do we have left? Do we still trust in God and cling to Him?

The writer of Habakkuk 3:17-18 implies that although all "props" would be taken away and everything seemingly out of control, yet he would rejoice in the Lord and joy in the God of his salvation. He declared the Lord God would be his strength and God "will make my feet like hinds' feet, and he will make me to walk upon mine high places" (v.19).

Do we find God enough in our hard situations? Or do we rebel against Him when we face a challenge, as the Children of Israel did (Numbers 14:1-10)? When the going gets tough, do we disregard God's Word and do things our own way as Moses did at Meribah (Numbers 20:7-12)?

God wants us to find Him enough in all of life.

PRAYER: Oh God, help me to see You as being enough in my life when everything seems wrong and out of control.

Related verses: Psalm 26:2, 40:5, 118:8, 125:1-2

NO CONDEMNATION

"There is therefore now no condemnation to them which are in Christ Jesus, who walk not after the flesh, but after the Spirit." Romans 8:1

A wilderness experience often brings with it condemnation, either from self or from our enemy, Satan. Satan's condemning words say: "You are a failure. A Christian shouldn't be in the wilderness." Self-condemnation says: "I'm letting my family and others down. I'm no good for anything."

If we allow these thoughts to occupy our minds, we can get to the place where we believe these condemnations are from God. In everything we hear there's condemnation. Soon we become confused and don't know how to discern what word is from God.

There is a difference in self or Satan's condemnation and conviction from God through the Holy Spirit. When it's self or Satan's condemnation, we feel pressed down and guilt-ridden, and that we can never change. Life seems hopeless and continues to look dark. But when God convicts us, we hear a focus on the problem or act, accompanied by a sense of His love. We know we can be different. There is no condemnation, only light and hope.

When we're in the wilderness and feel condemnation, let's remember condemnation doesn't come from God, so we don't have to accept it. We can have confidence that if there's something in our lives that needs changing, God will show us in a way that includes hope and a knowing He loves us and will lead us to wholeness.

PRAYER: Lord God, enable me to reject the condemnation that is causing darkness in my soul, and to trust You to show me what needs changing. Thank You for your love.

Related verses: Isaiah 50:9; John 3:16-18, 5:24; Romans 8:33-39

THE WAY

"And thine ears shall hear a word behind thee, saying, This is the way, walk ye in it, when ye turn to the right hand, and when ye turn to the left." Isaiah 30:21

When we're in the wilderness, we sometimes feel as though God doesn't care about us anymore. We become discouraged because it seems God isn't guiding us as He did before we entered the wilderness.

But our God is a gracious, loving God. He doesn't show us the way to salvation and then let us on our own to find our way from that time forth. Rather, He promises His leading and guiding every step of the way. He says in Isaiah 30:21 if we get off the path, He will tell us the way again. It's so reassuring to know God will help us find our way. It's also reassuring that He is guiding us continually (Isaiah 58:11) and He will be our guide forever (Psalm 48:14). With promises such as these, we can go through life without fear of straying from God's way and we can live with the joy that His guidance is always available.

PRAYER: O God, thank You that I can depend on Your guidance and for the reassurance this knowledge gives me.

Related verses: Psalm 31:3, 32:8, 63:1-8; Isaiah 58:11; John 16:13

BLAHNESS

"*B*e merciful to me, Lord, for I am faint; O Lord, heal me, for my bones are in agony." Psalm 6:2 (NIV)

Usually in our wilderness times life is just plain "blah". Nothing excites. All is humdrum and bleak. By sheer force of will we do those things that have to be done, with no motivation to do more. We feel tired in body and weary of spirit.

Our blahness may be the result of something that happened and "hit us hard." Our minds and systems reeled under the impact of it all. Or perhaps there are circumstances in life that are hard and we have no control over them. Sometimes the weight of the situation becomes almost more than we can bear. Maybe we hurt for others who are hurting, or for loved ones who need God in their lives. Then there are all the expectations of others on our time, and we feel like saying, "Stop world and let me off!" Maybe we even feel like Job who said, "I loathe my life" (Job 10:1, NRSV).

Whatever the reason for our feelings of blahness or weariness, God is there for us. He is able to satisfy the weary soul and to replenish the sorrowful (Jeremiah 31:25). God wants us to persevere in these low times (Ephesians 6:18). Jesus understands our feelings (Hebrews 4:15) and wants to comfort us (2 Thessalonians 2:16-17).

PRAYER: O Lord, life is so blah right now. I seem to feel down all the time. Please enable me to persevere for Your honor and glory.

Related verses: Psalm 69; Isaiah 40:30-31; Acts 14:21-22; Hebrews 2:17-18

ABUNDANT LIFE

"... *I* am come that they might have life, and that they might have it more abundantly." John 10:10

Jesus came to give us abundant life. But when we're in the wilderness, we don't feel life is abundant.

What is the abundant life that Jesus came to give? Is it a life free of problems, hard times, temptations, and sorrow? Surely not, since Acts 14:22 says, "we must through much tribulation enter into the kingdom of God." Jesus, Himself, said, "In the world ye shall have tribulation" (John 16:33).

The abundant life is, first of all, being free from condemnation—the freedom we have in Christ Jesus from the law of sin and death (Romans 8:1-2). The abundant life is Jesus at the right hand of God interceding for us (v.34) and our knowing *nothing* can separate us from God's love (vv.35-39).

The abundant life is Jesus with us to the end of the world (Matthew 28:20) and God's promise to never leave or forsake us (Hebrews 13:5). The abundant life is having the assurance "God is our refuge and strength, a very present help in trouble" (Psalm 46:1).

The abundant life is having the power of the Holy Spirit, who makes us to abound in hope (Romans 15:13). That "hope is an anchor of the soul, both sure and stedfast" (Hebrews 6:19).

No, the abundant life is not freedom from hard times, but it is the power of God in us enabling us to be "troubled on every side, yet not distressed…perplexed, but not in despair; persecuted, but not forsaken; cast down, but not destroyed" (2 Corinthians 4:7-9).

PRAYER: Thank You, God, for the abundant life in Christ Jesus. I believe I have that life even if I don't *feel* it right now.

Related verses: Psalm 23; Psalm 91, 103; John 3:16, 5:24; 2 Peter 1:2-4

GRATITUDE

"Enter into his gates with thanksgiving, and into his courts with praise: be thankful unto him, and bless his name." Psalm 100:4

One of the things that helps us get through the wilderness faster is to praise God, count our blessings and thank God for them as we name them one by one. When we're feeling low, it's hard to feel gratitude, but when we really focus in on those things that are blessings (and we all have some) and thank God for them, it can change the tone of our feelings. God has blessed all of us with countless good things. Yes, there are hard things in all of our situations too, and if we keep our minds on them, we lose perspective and feel *all* of life is hard.

For starters, we can praise God for Who He is—the God above all gods who is always worthy of our praise no matter what. Then there are those many spiritual blessings—the fact that God loves us so much, Jesus' sacrifice for our sins—and on and on. There are also the physical blessings: food, clothing, shelter (maybe not exactly the kind we'd like to have, but blessings nonetheless). If we take the time and make the effort, we will find many things to be thankful for. An "attitude of gratitude" goes a long way toward alleviating negative and hopeless feelings.

PRAYER: Help me, God, to concentrate on my blessings instead of on the hard things in my life. Thank You so much for (name your blessings).

Related verses: Psalm 50:14-15, 95:1-6; Philippians 4:6-7; Colossians 2:6-7

WAIT ON THE LORD

"They that wait upon the Lord shall renew their strength; they shall mount up with wings as eagles; they shall run, and not be weary; and they shall walk, and not faint." (Isaiah 40:31)

People in the wilderness know feelings of weakness—both physical and spiritual, and feelings of not being able to rise above the things that are causing them to be in the wilderness. They also know feelings of immobility—they are unmotivated and unproductive. Life is just one big "heavy" that causes weariness and feelings of despair.

God knows how we feel, and He knows we don't want to feel that way. He knows our longings to be out of the wilderness and our desire to feel normal again. But God has His timing for us to come out of the wilderness. Usually there is a period of waiting.

Waiting is difficult, but Isaiah 40:31 says if we wait upon the Lord, our strength will be renewed. We will be able to rise above our low and desperate feelings. We will again be able to live life normally without being weary of living. And we will be able to serve God and others without feelings of despair and wanting to give up.

God gives power to the faint and strength to the weak (Isaiah 40:29). Let's turn our minds to God and wait upon Him, trusting He will fulfill His promise to us.

PRAYER: Help me, Lord, to wait upon You for strength and the ability to rise above this hard time.

Related verses: Psalm 25:1-5, 27:14, 37:7, 62:1-8;

GRACE

"*For* by grace you have been saved through faith, and this is not your own doing; it is the gift of God..." Ephesians 2:8 (NRSV)

Grace! What a marvelous word! It's what we all need because "there is none righteous, no not one" (Romans 3:10). Grace is the only hope we have since we "all have sinned and come short of the glory of God" (Romans 3:23). 1 John 1:9 says, "If we confess our sins, He is faithful and just to forgive us our sins and to cleanse us from all unrighteousness." When we have been forgiven, God remembers our sins no more (Jeremiah 31:34). Then why do *we* remember them? If *God* doesn't remember them, *who* is it that keeps bringing our sins back to haunt us? It is our enemy, Satan.

When Satan hounds us with the "if onlys" and "I should/shouldn't haves," grace is our refuge. None of us *deserves* to be saved, but God loves us so much that He gives us His unmerited favor and saves us anyway. When Satan tempts us to despair because of the bad things we have done and the good things we should have done, we must remember it's by grace *only* that we are saved. Our salvation is a gift from God—a gift of His grace, no matter what our sins have been. When Jesus was nailed to the cross, our sins were nailed there with Him. Let's not take them down and bind ourselves with them again.

PRAYER: O God, I've repented of my sins. Help me to accept Your grace and forgiveness and to resist Satan when he tries to bring those sins back on me.

Related verses: Romans 3:23-26; Ephesians 2:4-8

JOY FOR THE JOURNEY

"... *T*he joy of the Lord is your strength." Nehemiah 8:10

When we're in the wilderness we feel as though we'll never know joy again. All we feel is sadness, emptiness, and hopelessness. But these are only *feelings*. True, we're not happy, but joy goes deeper than happiness.

Happiness is determined by what's happening in our lives, but joy is a fruit of the Holy Spirit, given to us by God. Joy is not determined by outward circumstances, but by what God has done for us. Even when we're feeling "down" we can rejoice in the Lord and exalt in God because "he has clothed me with the garments of salvation, he has covered me with the robe of righteousness" (Isaiah 61:10, NRSV). The fact of God loving us so much that even when we were lost in sin, He made us alive together with Christ, is cause to rejoice. We have much to joy about because we are saved by grace (Ephesians 2:4-5).

Our circumstances may change, life may become difficult and we may end up in the wilderness, but nothing changes what God has done for us by sending Jesus, His only Son, to die for us. No matter what our situation or how we feel, the fact that Jesus died in our place to set us free, gives cause for praise. As we offer this sacrifice of praise to God, it releases the joy that was bound by our low feelings. If we allow that joy of the Lord to well up, we will find it strengthens us and carries us through the wilderness.

PRAYER: O Lord, thank You for all You have done for me. Enable me to praise You and to feel the joy and strength You give.

Related verses: Psalm 28:7; Isaiah 12; Habakkuk 3:17-18; 2 Corinthians 6:10; Philippians 4:4

LONELY WALK

"... No man stood with me, but all men forsook me... notwithstanding the Lord stood with me, and strengthened me..." 2 Timothy 4:16-17

It can be lonely in the wilderness. Sometimes there's no one who really understands our situation. There may be people who can sympathize with our low feelings, but it may be that we don't know of *anyone* who has gone through what we're going through, so there's no one who can *really* understand. And even if there were, our situation may be such that we don't feel able to share with others because of exposing someone we love. These dynamics create a very lonely wilderness situation.

God, however, knows our situation. He is the only One who understands our every need, problem, and heartache. God is the only One who knows exactly what we're feeling and struggling with, and the only One who can bring healing, peace, and deliverance. God knows us better than we know ourselves. And God is with us every minute!

Healing for our lonely walk in the wilderness comes when we commune with God about our struggles. It is only when we bring our feelings, thoughts, motives, and temptations to Him and let the light of His healing presence cleanse and renew us, that we can become the persons He wants us to be.

PRAYER: Thank You, God, that You are with me constantly. Thank You that You know everything about my struggles. Please help me to sense Your presence in this lonely walk.

Related verses: Job 23:10; Psalm 31:7-8, 139:1-18

SAVED !!

"... *F*ear not: for I have redeemed thee, I have called thee by thy name; thou art mine." Isaiah 43:1

Some people have times in their lives when they doubt their salvation. This can happen in the wilderness. Satan, the father of lies, enjoys trying to trip us up with this temptation.

One thing that helps combat this temptation is to remind ourselves—and Satan—that it doesn't depend on anything *we* can do to determine our salvation. There's not a thing we can do to save ourselves. The only way we can be saved is by accepting what *Jesus* has done for us. He died on the cross to save us from our sins and it is only *His sacrifice* that has provided our way to heaven. We can never be "good enough" to earn our way there. But we can choose to believe God's Word that tells us not to fear because He has redeemed us and calls us by our name. We are *His*!!

PRAYER: Thank You, God, for providing my way to heaven. I have accepted Jesus' sacrifice for my sins and I choose to believe I am Your child—now and *always*.

Related verses: Isaiah 43:25, 44:22; John 3:16-17; Acts 2:21; Romans 10:9; Ephesians 2:8-9; Colossians 2:10; 2 Timothy 1:9; Titus 3:5; 1 John 4:4

COMPLETE IN JESUS

"And ye are complete in [Jesus], which is the head of all principality and power." Colossians 2:10

Sometimes in life we feel fragmented and fragile, and especially so when we're in the wilderness. But even though we have shattered and unstable feelings, we are told in Colossians 2:10 we are complete in Jesus. There is a center—a base—from which we operate and that center is Jesus, who never changes. Our wholeness lies in Him and He is all we need to be complete persons. Though hard situations and wilderness experiences cause us to feel "off-base," He continues to be our center. Our completeness in Him doesn't change with our feelings. He has done all that is necessary to make us complete persons, and that remains a fact we can always trust, even when our feelings can't be trusted.

PRAYER: Lord Jesus, in good times—and bad—help me to remember I am complete in You. Thank You for making my completeness possible.

Related verses: John 1:16; Ephesians 1:3

GOD'S COMPASSION

"As a father has compassion on his children, so the Lord has compassion on those who fear him; for he knows how we are formed, he remembers that we are dust." Psalm 103:13-14, (NIV)

Certain things can happen in our lives that trigger old regrets because of sins and failures, and even though we've been forgiven and have let go of them, we still feel down on ourselves. We may have hurt others in the past. Or we know we failed to follow God at different points along the way. We may even feel we're a hindrance to those people close to us. Because of our mistakes and failures we may be tempted to feel we've goofed up God's plan for our lives and the only thing we can do now is "put in time" for the remainder of our days on earth.

Let's take heart! Psalm 103:13-14 tells us the Lord has compassion on us—His children, and remembers we are human. And being human, we make mistakes. Even though we have failed in the past, God is still concerned about us and wants to direct our lives from here on. Psalm 121:8 (NRSV) says, "The Lord will keep your going out and your coming in from this time on and forevermore." God still loves us and has work for us to do. He still has a plan for our lives and wants to get us back into that plan. God can use our mistakes and failures for His glory, if we allow Him to do so.

PRAYER: Lord God, thank You for Your compassion. I give my mistakes and failures, along with the regrets, to You. Please use them for Your glory.

Related verses: Psalm 78:37-39, 86:15, 111:4, 112:4, 145:8; Lamentations 3:22-23; Micah 7:18-19 (NIV)

BRUISED

"... *It* pleased the Lord to bruise [Jesus]; he hath put him to grief..." Isaiah 53:10

Sometimes when we read or recall the story of Jesus' death, we forget this was God's plan. God knew long before that it would be necessary to bruise Jesus—"to put him to grief."

When Jesus was struggling with wanting to escape the horrors ahead, He reminded Himself it was for this purpose He was born. And He prayed God's name would be glorified (John 12:27-28). He submitted Himself to the will of His Father—to God's plan and purposes (Luke 22:41-42).

What about the hard times—the wilderness experiences in our own lives? Does God see there's need for us to be "bruised and put to grief" at times? How do we respond to our bruising and grief? None of us wants those times. We, like Jesus, would prefer not to go through hard times. But do we, like Jesus, pray God's name will be glorified through our suffering? Do we submit ourselves to God's will for us—to His plan and purposes for our lives? We would do well to follow Jesus' example when God sees it necessary to "bruise us" and "put us to grief."

PRAYER: Lord God, when You see fit to allow bruising and grief in my life, enable me to be submissive to Your will. And may Your name be glorified.

Related verses: Romans 5:3-5; 1 Peter 4:1-2, 5:10

PERFECT COUNSELOR

"*I* will bless the Lord who gives me counsel..." Psalm 16:7 (NRSV)

There are many counselors available today, and it seems as time goes on, we continue to need more. The problem is, there are all *kinds* of counselors. Some counselors lead people astray. We do well to use caution when seeking the service of counselors.

Where can we find the *perfect* Counselor, one who will never lead us astray? While there are many good Christian counselors, there is only One *perfect* Counselor, who is absolutely guaranteed to never lead us down a wrong path. That Counselor is the Lord. He is also the only Counselor who already knows everything about us, the only one who can be with us every moment—day and night, and the only one whose advice is always without charge. Isaiah 9:6 NIV) says Jesus is a Wonderful Counselor.

While it is sometimes necessary for us to seek help from a human counselor, God wants us to know Him as our *perfect* Counselor. He wants to guide us with His counsel (Psalm 73:24). He wants us to find counsel in His Word which is "a lamp to [our] feet and a light to [our] path" (Psalm 119:105). Yes, our best Counselor is God, who already knows "all the imaginations of the thoughts" (1 Chronicles 28:9). He wants to be our Counselor in bad times—and good.

PRAYER: Lord God, I want to know You as my perfect Counselor. Please lead me and guide me in this wilderness.

Related verses: Psalm 48:14; Proverbs 3:5-6, 16:3, 20:24; Isaiah 30:21; Jeremiah 10:23, 32:19

GOD WILL....

"Now the God of peace...Make you perfect in every good work to do his will, working in you that which is well pleasing in his sight, through Jesus Christ..." Hebrews 13:20-21

Life continues to be difficult. Our situation is the same, so there's always that nagging undercurrent of unrest trying to pull us down into its clutches. Maybe we're in a hard situation that causes us to feel trapped and thwarted, and we feel it will never change.

Whatever we face, God can help us endure. He can give us stability and peace in the worst kind of situation. He is the great "I WILL." He says, "I will bless thee..." (Genesis 12:2); "I will not fail thee..." (Joshua 1:5); "I will heal thee..." (2 Kings 20:5); "I will guide thee..." (Psalm 32:8); "I will help thee..." (Isaiah 41:10); "I will deliver thee..." (Psalm 50:15); "I will hold thine hand..." (Isaiah 42:6); "I will not forget thee..." (Isaiah 49:15); "I will comfort thee..." (Isaiah 66:13); "I will forgive thee..." (Jeremiah 31:34); "I will restore thee..." (Jeremiah 30:17).

Yes, through all of God's "I wills," He is making us perfect to do His will and working in us what is pleasing to Himself.

PRAYER: Thank You for all Your "I will" promises, God. May I be able to believe them so You can work Your will in me.

Related verses: Matthew 11:29; 2 Corinthians 3:5; Philippians 2:13

TRUE FAITH

"For we walk by faith, not by sight." 2 Corinthians 5:7

It takes hard situations to test and mature our faith. When life is going smoothly, it doesn't require much faith to believe God loves us and is doing His best for us. But let troubles and hard times come and "walking by faith and not by sight" takes on real meaning.

True faith isn't believing things will work out the way *we* want them to, or the way *we* think is best. True faith goes beyond that—to believing God will work things out *His* way, the way He knows is best for us. True faith says, as Shadrach, Meshach, and Abednego said in Daniel 3:17-18: "Our God whom we serve is able to deliver us…But if not [we will continue to serve Him]." True faith says with Job, "Though he slay me, yet will I trust in him" (Job 13:15). True faith recognizes feelings of hopelessness and despair, as the Psalmist did in Psalm 42, but still believes God's love and presence are there (v.8) even if they can't be felt. True faith says, as Jesus did, "Father, into thy hands I commend my spirit" (Luke 23:46) even when the feelings scream, "My God, my God, why hast thou forsaken me?" (Mark 15:34). True faith causes us to pray, believing God will answer in His own time and in His own way. True faith invites Jesus to come into our hard situations and walk with us through them. The grace, strength, and peace He gives us in the wilderness is often a greater miracle than His delivering us *from* our hard situation.

PRAYER: Thank You, God, for keeping me and enabling me to endure in this hard time.

Related verses: Acts 14:22; James 1:2-4; 1 Peter 1:7, 4:12-13

WAITING IS DIFFICULT

"Wait on the Lord: be of good courage, and he shall strengthen thine heart: wait, I say, on the Lord." Psalm 27:14

Waiting is so difficult—especially waiting for God's timing in our hard situations. Instead of continuing to give the people and circumstances in our lives to God for *His* changing, we find ourselves rushing ahead to move people to action or trying to remedy situations we feel have been that way long enough. And every time we do that, it turns out wrong and then we see God wants us to continue to leave bothersome people and circumstances in His hands.

We have to continually apply the Serenity Prayer which says, "God, grant me the serenity to accept the things I cannot change, the courage to change the things I can, and the wisdom to know the difference."

There are people and situations only God can change, but when God allows them to remain the same for so long, it's difficult to wait for Him to act. Sometimes we're tempted to want "out" of the hard situation. But God says, "Wait on [me]." If we wait, He will renew our strength. We will mount up with wings as the eagles. We will run and not be weary. We will walk and not faint (Isaiah 40:31).

PRAYER: O God, help me to wait!

Related verses: Psalm 25:5, 37:7; Lamentations 3:25-26; Micah 7:7

ABIDE IN JESUS

"Abide in me [Jesus], and I in you…" John 15:4

Our wilderness experience continues on and on. How can we endure and continue to be the person God wants us to be?

Our hope is found in John 15:4. We have to abide in Jesus and let Him abide in us. We cannot possibly bear the fruit of love, joy, peace, longsuffering, gentleness, goodness, faith, meekness and temperance (Galatians 5:22) unless we abide in Him. When we're in an on-going hard situation, one of the things we need most is patience. If our situation involves a difficult relationship, we also need love, longsuffering, and gentleness. In other hard situations including dealing with grief or a long-term health problem, we need joy, peace, faith, meekness, and temperance in addition to patience. Jesus makes it clear we can't produce good fruit unless we abide in Him.

Abide means "to stand fast; remain; to stay." It's not a now-and-then thing. If we abide in Jesus, we are in communication with Him continually. All during the day and night, we're aware of our need of His presence, help, strength, and grace. We depend on Him continuously to produce in us (by His Spirit) that fruit which we need at any particular time. Only as we abide in Jesus and allow Him to abide in us can we endure our wilderness situation and be the person God wants us to be.

PRAYER: Jesus, help me to abide—to stay—in You continually. I need Your Presence and Your power to produce Your fruit in me.

Related verses: John 15:5; Romans 7:24; 1 John 2:6, 28; 3:6, 24

BLESS THE LORD

"*E*very day will I bless [God]; and I will praise [His] name for ever and ever." Psalm 145:2

There are those days that start out good—and then something happens that threatens to undo us. Perhaps we put time and effort into helping someone and instead of appreciation, we get a critical remark. Or maybe there are unexpected changes or interruptions in our plans.

When difficult things threaten our peace, the best thing to do is immediately pray for the person or persons involved. Thank God for them. Ask God to bless them and to give you His love for them. Then begin to praise God and keep on praising Him until your peace is fully restored. When we do this, we bless God because we are following the instructions in His Word (Matthew 5:44). We also bless Him when we praise Him. Psalm 34:1 says, "I will bless the Lord at all times: his praise shall continually be in my mouth."

After we recognize the hurt and disappointment we feel because of the unexpected or difficult happening in our lives, we can choose to bless the Lord and praise Him instead of dwelling on our feelings. Continuing to think about our feelings or the actions of those people who caused us stress will destroy our peace and undo us. Blessing the Lord and praising Him will soothe our feelings, restore our peace and joy, and enable us to continue on undisturbed. The choice is ours.

PRAYER: Instead of dwelling on my feelings or on another person's actions, help me, Lord, to choose to bless You when someone hurts me or causes me disappointment.

Related verses: Psalm 63:3-6, 103:1-5, 145:9-12; Revelation 4:11

MATURITY

"… *U*ntil all of us come…to maturity, to the measure of the full stature of Christ." Ephesians 4:13 (NRSV)

We want to live victoriously in our wilderness situation. We want to rise above our circumstances and be able to run and not be weary and walk and not faint (Isaiah 40:31). And for awhile, we do. But just when we think we've finally learned to cast our cares on God, to trust Him, to depend on Him, to take everything in stride and to love unconditionally, an unexpected "curve in the road" catches us off guard and we end up in the "junk yard." Or so we think! We get discouraged and wonder if we'll ever be mature Christians.

Let's take courage. The Bible indicates the Christian life is one of *growth*. The Apostle Paul tells us to "*grow* in grace, and in the knowledge of our Lord and Saviour Jesus Christ" (2 Peter 3:18). Ephesians 4:15 speaks of our growing up into Christ in all things. Even Jesus (Who was God in the flesh) "*increased* in wisdom…and in favor with God and man" (Luke 2:52).

So let's not get discouraged when we seem to take five steps forward and three steps back. We're learning and growing even at *those* times. Perhaps we just need a "refresher course" along the way.

PRAYER: Lord God, when I'm tempted to be discouraged because of failure, remind me that You don't expect me to know everything at once.

Related verses: Proverbs 9:9-10; Isaiah 29:19; Luke 17:5; 1 Thessalonians 3:12, 4:9-10; 2 Thessalonians 1:3; Ephesians 4:13-15

FIX OUR HEARTS

"My heart is fixed, O God, my heart is fixed: I will sing and give praise." Psalm 57:7

What is the condition of our heart in the wilderness? Is it fixed (steadfast) on God for sure—or fixed depending on what happens?

When unexpected events come into our lives, such as interruptions or our plans changed, our natural inclination is to fret and fume. But God knows what is happening. Could it be He wants us to do something else right now or He has something different in mind for our day?

God sees the whole picture and knows just the right time for everything that needs to be done. When we're not sure what's happening or what we should do at a given time, do we stop to acknowledge God and ask Him to direct us (Proverbs 3:5-6)?

It's so hard to "hang loose" and trust God when we think we should be doing certain things "now." We tend to forget our time isn't really ours, but God's, and He will give us the time to do whatever He wants us to do—*when* he wants it done.

We can choose how we react and respond to interruptions and unexpected changes in plans. When we choose to accept the situation as a challenge, fix our hearts on God and give Him praise, it opens the way for God to direct us. It also opens our minds and hearts to hear His direction.

PRAYER: Lord God, I don't know what's happening nor what You want me to do.I choose to fix my heart on You, give You praise, and trust You to direct me.

Related verses: Psalm 108:1, 112:7

LOVE IS A CHOICE

"*I* give you a new commandment, that you love one another. Just as I have loved you, you also should love one another." John 13:34 (NRSV)

Are you at odds with a person close to you? Are there things you don't like about your situation and when you tried to talk to the other person about those things, you couldn't seem to get through to them? And now you don't feel love for that person?

Love is a choice. Even when we don't *feel* love, we can choose to do acts of love and to speak words of love. We can go on the fact that we *do* love them, even if we don't *feel* love. Jesus said in order to be children of God, we are to "Love your enemies, bless them that curse you, do good to them that hate you, and pray for them which despitefully use you, and persecute you" (Matthew 5:44-45).

We can choose to "heap coals of fire" on the heads of those who are hard to love (Romans 12:20). And we can ask God to restore our *feelings* of love.

We can't change our feelings, but when we choose to show love and persist in obeying God's command to love, He will honor our obedience and change our feelings. Maybe not right away, but it will happen. When that happens, it's up to *us* to nurture the positive feelings by continuing to allow the Holy Spirit to produce in us the fruit of love, longsuffering, gentleness, and goodness (Galatians 5:22). The choice is ours whether or not we obey.

PRAYER: Lord God, I don't have any feelings of love for
_____. Show me how to obey you by doing acts of love for
_____. And please restore my *feelings* of love.

Related verses: Luke 6:32-36; John 13:35; 1 Corinthians 13

WHY THE WILDERNESS?

"*H*e brought me up also out of an horrible pit, out of the miry clay, and set my feet upon a rock, and established my goings." Psalm 40:2

There were men of God in the Bible who found themselves in the depths. Job was a righteous man and yet he came to the place where his despair caused him to ask why he'd been born and to wish God would destroy him (Job 6:8-9). At one point, Elijah, a godly prophet, also longed for death (1 Kings 19:4). The Apostle Paul served God faithfully and yet there were times when he felt so burdened—so crushed—he despaired of living (2 Corinthians 1:8).

Why does God allow His people to sink so low? We find one good reason in 2 Corinthians 1:9: so we don't trust *in ourselves* but in *God*. God wants to strengthen our faith in Him. God also allows wilderness experiences so we learn to call on Him immediately when we *begin* to sink as Peter did (Matthew 14:8-30). Instead of believing Satan's lies and dwelling on our negative feelings, God wants us to believe His Word and live by the facts. Instead of allowing our fears to fester and grow, God wants us to seek Him so He can deliver us from our fears (Psalm 34:4).

When we wait patiently for God, He will hear us and bring us up out of the miry bog and set our feet upon a rock. He will make our steps secure (Psalm 40:1-2, NRSV).

PRAYER: O God, I know You have reasons for allowing me to experience the wilderness. I trust You to bring me out of this horrible pit and to make my steps secure.

Related verses: Psalm 37:39-40, 91:15, 130:1-2,5

JESUS, OUR TREASURE

"**B**ut we have this treasure in earthen vessels, that the excellency of the power may be of God, and not of us." 2 Corinthians 4:7

As long as all is well, we're able to handle life by ourselves. But when certain things happen and life becomes difficult, what do we do? Fall apart? Go under?

We need more than our own human resources when the going gets tough. We need a special power from God to keep us going—the power that is Jesus—the treasure in our human bodies. The Apostle Paul says that with the glorious power within, "We are pressed on every side by troubles, but not crushed and broken. We are perplexed because we don't know why things happen as they do, but we don't give up and quit. We are hunted down, but God never abandons us. We get knocked down, but we get up again and keep going" (2 Corinthians 4:7-9, LIVING).

The only way we can survive hardships is to depend on God's power and not on our own. Of ourselves, we are weak, but it's when we feel weak that God is strong for us. His strength is made perfect in our weakness. It is in our weakness that His grace becomes sufficient (2 Corinthians 12:9).

It is only when we abide in Jesus and allow Him to abide in us (John 15:5), that we realize God's power. It's God's power that strengthens us and enables us to have patience and longsuffering with joyfulness when life is hard (Colossians 1:11).

PRAYER: Lord God, strengthen me with Your might and power in this hard time.

Related verses: Jeremiah 32:17; 2 Corinthians 6:4-7; Ephesians 3:20, 6:10

TIME WITH JESUS

"Now when they saw the boldness of Peter and John, and perceived that they were unlearned and ignorant men, they marvelled; and they took knowledge of them, that they had been with Jesus." Acts 4:13

Often the person in the wilderness battles low self-esteem. One thing that can cause low self-esteem is not having the education friends and acquaintances have.

Not everyone has the opportunity for a "higher education." But there is one education *all* of us have access to. We can be taught by *Jesus*. Peter and John were "unlearned and ignorant" men, yet people were amazed at their words and actions and recognized they had been with Jesus.

The Apostle Paul told the Corinthians his speech and preaching weren't with "enticing words of man's wisdom," but were through the Spirit's power (1 Corinthians 2:4). He didn't want his hearers' faith to "stand in the wisdom of men, but in the power of God" (v.5).

All of us have the same opportunity to spend time with Jesus that Peter, John, and Paul had, and to let Jesus teach us. The education Jesus gives is the very best and is a necessity both for life in this world and for our journey to heaven. Our self-worth is not determined by our formal education, but by our worth to God. We are worth so much to God that He, Himself, desires to give us the best education. But in order for God to do that, we *must* spend time with Him and in His Word.

PRAYER: God, I desire the education only You can give. As I spend time with You, help me to be Your willing and obedient student.

Related verses: Proverbs 3:5-6; 1 Corinthians 1:27-29; 2 Corinthians 4:7

WHEN WE SIN

"*I*f we confess our sins, he is faithful and just to forgive us our sins, and to cleanse us from all unrighteousness." 1 John 1:9

How terrible we feel when we sin against God! We don't want to fail Him or disobey Him, but suddenly we realize that's exactly what we've done. How could we have done such a thing? We feel like a failure.

Moses must have experienced the same thoughts and feelings when he sinned against God. After serving God so faithfully all those years in the wilderness, he "blew it" (Numbers 20:7-11). When the children of Israel needed water in the wilderness, God told Moses to speak to the rock and it would bring forth water. But instead of *speaking* to the rock, Moses *struck* it with his rod (v. 11).

Why did Moses disobey God? Verse 10 indicates he was frustrated with the Children of Israel. Was striking the rock Moses' way of releasing his frustration? Or didn't Moses think through his action beforehand?

Are we like Moses? When we sin, is it because of frustration in our lives? Do we sometimes decide our way is better than God's way? Do we fail to take time to discern the possible consequences of our actions?

The wonderful thing is that even though God had to punish Moses by not allowing Him entrance into the Promised Land (v. 12), God didn't negate Moses' previous work for Him. And God still allowed Moses to continue as leader of the Children of Israel. In spite of his failure, at his death Moses was called the "servant of the Lord" (Deuteronomy 34:5).

What a comfort to know when we sin, God doesn't cast us off and relegate us to the "trash heap," but forgives us and continues to use us in His service.

PRAYER: Thank You, God, for Your mercy and forgiveness when I sin. And thank You that You continue to use me for Your honor and glory.

Related verses: Psalm 32:1, 86:5, 130:3-4; Isaiah 44:22

CONVINCED

"… *I* know whom I have believed, and am convinced that he is able to guard what I have entrusted to him for that day." 2 Timothy 1:12 (NIV)

I have trusted my life to God. If I have given Him *all* of my life, it means whatever happens is in His hands—now and always—until I die. There may be wilderness experiences and I think I won't make it, but I have to remember I trusted my life to God and He is able to guard what I've entrusted to Him.

I may not *feel* God is able, but that doesn't change the fact that He *is* able. My steps are ordered by the Lord and He delights in my way. Even though I may fall along the way, I won't be utterly cast down because the Lord upholds me with His hand (Psalm 37:23-24). He will see me through the "down" times—the wilderness experiences. Psalm 138:8 (NRSV) says the Lord will fulfill His purpose for me and His love for me is steadfast and endures forever.

The Apostle Paul said he is "convinced" God is able to keep what he's entrusted to Him. He arrived at that certainty by going through hard times. Is it possible God is allowing our wilderness experience so we will be convinced of His ability? God wants our absolute trust in Him to be from first-hand knowledge—not from someone else's word. How will we know for ourselves God is able, unless we experience it? If we're convinced God is able, then we won't lose our faith in Him when we find ourselves in the wilderness.

PRAYER: Lord, I know You are able to keep me always. Please work out Your purpose for me, even in the wilderness.

Related verses: Jeremiah 32:17; John 17:11, 15; Romans 8:38-39; 2 Thessalonians 3:3; Jude 24

IN THE VALLEY

"... *I*n this world you will have trouble. But take heart! I have overcome the world."John 16:33 (NIV)

Being in the wilderness (valley) is hard. And yet, there are some good things about the valley. The best view of the mountain is from the valley. It's only in the valley that we can see the majesty of the mountain and appreciate its beauty. It's only in the valley that truths we heard on the mountaintop become real to us. We don't really learn the lessons of trusting God, the sacrifice of praise, patience, and especially endurance until we're in the valley. It's only in the valley that we come to the place of being fully persuaded (sure) God is able to keep what we have committed to Him (2 Timothy 1:12). If it weren't for the valleys, we would never learn to walk by faith and not by sight (2 Corinthians 5:7) or to live by the facts (2 Corinthians 1:20) instead of our feelings. It's only in the valley we learn we can depend on His "fear not, for I am with you, be not dismayed, for I am your God" and on His promises to give us His strength, help, and upholding (Isaiah 41:10). It's in the valley we experience God as our "refuge and strength, a very present help in trouble" (Psalm 46:1).

As much as we dislike the valleys (wildernesses) of our lives, they are as necessary as the mountaintops.

PRAYER: Lord, thank You for the valleys of life, but please hold me tightly when I'm in them.

Related verses: Isaiah 43:19-20; Jeremiah 32:17

HOPE IN THE LORD

"*B*e strong and take heart, all you who hope in the Lord." Psalm 31:24 (NIV)

Life in the wilderness can get so heavy. If we had only *one* hard thing to cope with at a time, it would be easier. But it seems many hard things come at once. Someone once said, "They told me there would be days like this, but they didn't tell me they would come in bunches like bananas."

Additional hard things are more difficult to bear if we're already in a trying situation and feeling fragile. With the extra burdens, we can reach a place of hopelessness. We may not have hope our situation will ever be different. We may feel hopeless that our problems will be solved in a good way, if at all. And when we're in the wilderness, we may not have hope of ever feeling better emotionally.

But there *is* a hope we can have even in the wilderness. God is a God of hope and when we believe Him, He fills us with joy and peace and the Holy Spirit makes us abound in hope (Romans 15:13). The Psalmist knew about the hope that is in God. In Psalm 42:11 he tells his own soul to hope in God and then in faith says, "for I shall yet praise him." The Psalmist recognized God as the health of his countenance (Healer of his emotions).

Let's choose to believe God and hope in Him and He will strengthen our heart.

PRAYER: O God, I feel so hopeless. Please enable me to hope in You. I need You to strengthen my heart.

Related verses: Psalm 16:8-9, 33:22, 38:15, 39:7, 71:14; Psalm 130:1-6, 146:5; Lamentations 3:24-26

CONSTANT YIELDING

"... *T*he Great, the Mighty God, the Lord of hosts, is his name, Great in counsel, and mighty in work..." Jeremiah 32:18-19

The only way we can make it in the wilderness is to have a deep, abiding trust in God. When we have that kind of trust, we can yield ourselves and each hard thing—as it comes—to God, with the confidence He is strong enough to keep us and mighty enough to work out those things that would pull us down. We yield to God knowing that by His power within us, He can "accomplish abundantly far more than all we can ask or imagine" (Ephesians 3:20, NRSV). There are no works like God's works (Psalm 86:8).

Yielding to God and believing Him is not a one-time thing. We have to *continually* yield to Him and state our belief that He is able to work in our situation. If we don't put our confidence in Him continually—and especially when a hard thing happens—we will likely remain in the wilderness.

If we find ourselves in the wilderness, the only way out is to yield ourselves and our problems to God and believe He is strong enough to work in our behalf. We have to begin to *constantly* turn our worries over to Him and let them there (Philippians 4:6-7). The way out of the wilderness may be long and hard, but if we persist in yielding to God, giving our worries to Him and believing He is working in us, we will make it.

PRAYER: Mighty God, help me to truly believe You are Almighty and able to work in me and in my situation. I yield to You.

Related verses: Exodus 15:11; Psalm 50:1, 86:7-10, 91:1, 106:2; Jeremiah 33:3; Nahum 1:7

TEARS ARE OK

"*J*esus wept."John 11:35

When we're in the wilderness we may find tears are often a part of our life, even when we don't want to cry. The least little thing brings tears. We may cry at the "wrong" times and are embarrassed or ashamed.

Jeremiah, known as the weeping prophet, wasn't ashamed of his tears (Jeremiah 9:1; 13:17; 14:17). Finally after all his weeping, God told him to stop crying because Jeremiah's work would be rewarded and God's people would come back from the land of the enemy (Jeremiah 31:16).

The Psalmist knew times of crying (Psalm 6:6, 42:3). In Psalm 56:8 the Psalmist asks God to put his tears into God's bottle. We're told in Psalm 126:5, "They that sow in tears shall reap in joy." Even Jesus cried in the hard times of his life (Hebrews 5:7-8).

Tears are healing. They bring release from inner tension. Tears wash the windows of the soul so it can see through to God. God recognizes tears (Isaiah 38:4-5). In His timing, He brings deliverance (Psalm 116:8). Let's accept our tears as therapy and allow them to do their healing work.

PRAYER: Thank You, God, that You have given us tears as a release in frustration and pain. I offer my tears to You and pray You will bring me healing through them.

Related verses: Esther 8:3-4; Job 16:20; Mark 9:24; Luke 7:37-38,44; Acts 20:19,31

LIGHTEN UP

"A cheerful heart is a good medicine, but a downcast spirit dries up the bones." Proverbs 17:22 (NRSV)

When hard times come, we tend to let life get too heavy. We mull over our problems and worry our way through each day, until we end up in the wilderness.

When this happens, we need to start making effort to "lighten up." It may mean looking for things we can laugh at: jokes, funny sayings, cute child or grandchild remarks, and then making effort to actually laugh at them. Proverbs 17:22 tells us a downcast spirit dries up the bones. It's a vicious cycle: we become downcast and then our body feels tense and sort of shrivels as we withdraw into our problems, which in turn makes us feel worse mentally. We have to make effort to get our body moving. We can take brisk walks. We can dance—or skip—around the room while we listen to praise music and sing along, making effort to keep our mind on the words. As we skip around, we can offer the sacrifice of praise to God. The two together are a good release for the spirit because the physical and emotional are closely related.

We may not feel better immediately after we make efforts at lightening up, but if we persist, the results will begin to show. We can't change our own feelings, but God can use our efforts in His timing to give us the "garment of praise for the spirit of heaviness" (Isaiah 61:3).

PRAYER: Lord God, please give me the will and strength to work at lightening up. I trust You to give me the garment of praise in Your timing.

Related verses: Psalm 119:28; Proverbs 12:25, 15:13; 1 Peter 1:5-7

HYPOCRITICAL?

"*A* merry heart maketh a cheerful countenance: but by sorrow of the heart the spirit is broken." Proverbs 15:13

Some people in the wilderness think they shouldn't make effort to "lighten up" because "that's just not me if I praise God, skip around, or make myself laugh at something when I'm feeling low, and I'm being hypocritical."

But wait! Let's look at who is actually being hypocritical. When we're feeling normal, we praise and thank God. We believe and go on the facts and promises of God's Word. We walk with purpose and a spring in our step, and laugh at funny things. So which one is being hypocritical: the person who is feeling low but remains true to their *real* self by making effort to praise God, to walk with a skip, to find things to laugh at, to sing along with praise and worship songs, and who chooses to go on the promises of God's Word even though the *feelings* aren't there—or the person who gives in to their low feelings and doesn't make effort to lighten up by doing those things they would normally do?

The person who gives in to their low feelings and acts accordingly is the one who is being hypocritical. Being willing to be true to the "real me" and persisting in it when we're feeling low, gives God a framework in which to work to bring our feelings back to normal. It also enables Him to give us perspective of our situation and the people in it. He can bring us back to the place where we once again believe with our head—and our heart—the facts of the Word and promises of

God (2 Peter 1:4). When, in low times, we affirm the *fact* of our belief (our normal self *does* believe), the *feelings* will eventually follow.

PRAYER: O God, enable me to be true to my *real* self and to act accordingly.

Related verses: Psalm 5:11-12; Psalm 13, 42:11; 2 Corinthians 1:20;

TESTED

"*Prove me, O Lord, and try me; test my heart and mind.*" Psalm 26:2 (NRSV)

God has allowed this situation in which we're being sorely tested. It's working on our pride and the self in us. Oh yes, we've experienced testing many times before, but this particular situation is even worse because it involves our pride. For awhile, the situation was mostly hidden and it wasn't quite as hard. But now that it's exposed, our struggle with pride is greater.

What do people think of me? Do they think I'm lax? Do they think I don't care? Do they think less of me, now that they know? The self in me wants to hide, to cop out, or at least to shout, "This isn't *me!*" This isn't the way *I* want the situation to be!"

God is using this situation to get rid of our pride and to test us. God wants to know if we'll be faithful to Him in these hard circumstances, even though we don't like them. Even though they cause us grief. God wants to see if we will yield to Him and accept what we can't change. God is watching to see if we'll put blame on someone else—or love them unconditionally. Will we choose to seek God's grace, strength, and peace in our situation? God allows hard situations and wilderness experiences to test us, as He did the Children of Israel—to humble us, and to prove us, to know what's in our hearts, whether or not we'll keep His Words (Deuteronomy 8:2).

PRAYER: Help me, God, to pass this test.

Related verses: Psalm 139:23-24; Proverbs 17:3; Hebrews 11:17; James 1:12; 1 Peter 4:12-13

VULNERABLE

"*B*e careful—watch out for attacks from Satan, your great enemy..." 1 Peter 5:8 (THE LIVING BIBLE)

When we're in the wilderness, we can become extremely vulnerable to outside forces. Satan knows our vulnerability and uses every advantage to bring us down through our minds. Peter tells us to be careful (and vigilant) and watch for Satan's attacks. Just prior to this warning, Peter tells us to let God have all our worries and cares, for He is always thinking about us and watching everything that concerns us (1 Peter 5:7, LIVING).

It's fitting that the warning about Satan's attacks follows the advice to let God have all our worries and cares. If we don't give God our cares and worries, we become vulnerable to Satan. When we try to carry our own cares and work out our problems ourselves, we become heavy in spirit and Satan knows how to come in and cause our feelings to sink lower and lower. He speaks hopelessness and despair, and even tries to make us lose faith in God and what God is able to do for us. Once we let Satan get his foot in the door in one area, it's easier for him to take over in another—and another. But 1 Peter 5:9 (THE LIVING BIBLE) tells us what to do when Satan attacks. We're told to stand firm and trust the Lord. 1 Peter 5:9 (KJV) says to resist Satan steadfast in the faith. We have to do spiritual warfare (James 4:7) and set our will to start casting our cares and anxieties on God and leave them there.

PRAYER: Thank You, God, that You care for me. Help me to cast my cares upon You and to resist Satan.

Related verses: Matthew 4:10 (NRSV), 26:41; Luke 18:1; Philippians 4:6-7 (NIV)

ENDURE

"... *E*ndure hardness, as a good soldier of Jesus Christ." 2 Timothy 2:3

Life is hard—there's no doubt about it! But that's what we're told it would be. Acts 14:22 says, "we must through much tribulation enter into the kingdom of God."

James wrote about how the prophets were such examples of "suffering affliction, and of patience" and says, "we count them happy which endure" (James 5:10-11). Paul endured many persecutions and afflictions but said, "out of them all the Lord delivered me" (2 Timothy 3:11). Abraham patiently endured and obtained the promise (Hebrews 6:15). Jesus, Himself, became perfect through sufferings (Hebrews 2:10). He endured the cross (Hebrews 12:2).

We are called to be good soldiers of Jesus Christ. But it's difficult to endure. We feel like giving in, copping out, quitting the fight. Sometimes we feel we can't "hang in there" any longer. Hebrews 12:3 (NRSV) says we're to consider Jesus who endured such hostility against himself from sinners, so we won't grow weary or lose heart.

How do we learn endurance? By *enduring*. And after all the *enduring*—then what? "After you have suffered for a little while, the God of all grace, who has called you to his eternal glory in Christ, will himself restore, support, strengthen, and establish you" (1 Peter 5:10, NRSV).

In this time in the wilderness, take heart! Determine to endure and God will restore and establish you in His timing.

PRAYER: Sustainer God, please help me to endure in this hard situation. I believe Youare supporting and strengthening me and You will restore and establish me.

Related verses: 2 Thessalonians 1:4-5; 2 Timothy 4:5; Hebrews 10:32-36 (NRSV)

ACCEPT OURSELVES

"*My* soul, wait thou only upon God; for my expectation is from him." Psalm 62:5

When we're in the wilderness, it's easy to fall into the trap of feeling down on ourselves for not being able to pull ourselves out. We are told by well-meaning persons who have never been through the wilderness experience, we "have to snap out of it." That makes us feel all the more guilty.

The fact is: we can't change our own feelings. And to feel down on ourselves for not being able to do so only sends us deeper into the wilderness. We have to accept ourselves where we are and believe it's alright to be at this place for now, knowing and *believing* we won't always be here and God will bring us "out into a wealthy place" (Psalm 66:12). We need to remind ourselves often that "this too shall pass."

Instead of blaming ourselves for getting into the wilderness and feeling down on ourselves for not being able to get ourselves out, we would do well to follow the example of the Psalmist when he was in the depths. He cried unto the Lord and then waited for God and hoped in His word (Psalm 130:1, 5). God is the One who helps us when we're feeling low (Psalm 116:6). He will work in our lives, enabling us both to will and to do of His good pleasure (Philippians 2:13).

PRAYER: Help me, Lord, to accept myself where I am and trust You to change my feelings.

Related verses: Psalm 27:14, 37:7, 116:7-8, 123:2

CRY OUT TO GOD

"The eyes of the Lord are upon the righteous, and his ears are open unto their cry." Psalm 34:15

In the wilderness we can feel the gamut of emotions including fear, anxiety, discouragement, darkness, distress, rejection, alienation, and much more. When the Psalmist experienced these feelings, he cried out to God. He asked God to hear his cry (Psalm 17:1, 27:7, 28:1-2, 39:12, 119:145-149, 141:1, 142:6). At one point after he pleads with God to hear his prayer (102:1), the Psalmist tells God his heart is smitten and withered like grass so that he forgets to eat (v.4). In Psalm 88:3 the Psalmist tells God his soul is full of troubles and he feels he's near death. He says he has no strength and he's in the "lowest pit, in darkness, in the deeps" (vv.4, 6), his companions have left him (v.8), and he feels God is hiding His face from him (v.14).

In one of his experiences, the Psalmist was tempted to distrust God (Psalm 77:7-9), but he still cried unto the Lord in his trouble (vv.1-2). He said when he cried unto the Lord, the Lord heard him (Psalm 18:6, 31:21-22, 66:16-20) and sustained him (Psalm 3:4-5), healed him (30:2), delivered him from all his fears (34:4), saved him out of all his troubles (v.6) and strengthened him in his soul (138:3).

What does all this mean for us? Simply this: when we're in the wilderness and cry out to God and depend on Him as the Psalmist did, God will do for us what He did for the Psalmist.

PRAYER: O Lord, hear my cry in this wilderness. Help me to wait patiently for You to respond to me as You did to the Psalmist.

Related verses: Psalm 5:2, 28:6-7, 34:17, 40:1, 55:16-17, 62:8, 65:2, 107:19, 145:19

COME APART AND REST

"...[Jesus] said…Come ye yourselves apart into a desert place, and rest awhile." Mark 6:31

We read Jesus' words in Mark 6:31 and think, *How I wish I could rest awhile*. In our busy lives there's rarely a chance for long periods of rest, so we have to "make do" with a bit here and a bit there. Taking five minutes to be quiet now and then throughout the day will help greatly. We have to do that with feeding our souls also. We can sit down for those five minutes of rest, pick up a Christian magazine or devotional book (or the Bible) and catch five minutes of spiritual food. That will often be enough to keep us going until our next "break."

Psalm 23:2-3 says the Lord makes us lie down in green pastures; he leads us beside still waters; he restores our souls. The Lord can do that for us when we take even short breaks to rest. In our hectic lives, we have to give God the chance to bring rest and restoration to our inner selves. Failing to do so may be the cause of our being in the wilderness.

Jesus knew the importance of our taking time to come to Him. He says in Matthew 11:28 (NRSV), "Come unto me, all you that are weary and are carrying heavy burdens, and I will give you rest." Let's take the time to heed His words.

PRAYER: Lord Jesus, thank You for the rest You give us. Remind me often to "come apart and rest awhile" even if I can do so for only a short period of time.

Related verses: Psalm 116:7; Matthew 11:28-30

FEAR NOT!

"... *D*o not fear, for I have redeemed you; I have called you by name, you are mine." Isaiah 43:1 (NRSV)

Fear is a dreadful enemy. It can cause us to enter the wilderness and once there, it hounds us unmercifully. Things that would normally cause little concern seem like mountains when we're in the wilderness. But God says to us: "Do not fear…you are mine…When you pass through the waters, I will be with you; and through the rivers, they shall not overwhelm you" (Isaiah 43:1-2 (NRSV). What a comfort those words are when we're feeling overwhelmed and as though we're about to drown. And God doesn't give us those promises only for a one-time situation. He says to us, "even to your old age I am he, and even when you turn gray I will carry you. I have made, and I will bear; I will carry and will save" (Isaiah 46:4 (NRSV). No matter how many times we go through the wilderness, God will not forget us (Isaiah 49:15). And nothing can separate us from the love of God (Romans 8:38-39).

When we're in the wilderness, let's remember we are God's and He is right with us no matter how we feel. He will not let us "drown." He promises to carry us always and to save us. Just as He lifted up and carried His people long ago (Isaiah 63:9, NRSV), He will lift *us* up and carry us.

PRAYER: Lord God, I thank You that I am Yours. Please take away my fear and help me to trust You to deliver me from this wilderness.

Related verses: Psalm 27:1,3; Isaiah 41:10

THROUGH THE NIGHT

"You will not fear the terror of the night..." Psalm 91:5 (NRSV)

Nights in the wilderness can be long and difficult. Some people don't have trouble sleeping when they're in the wilderness, but others dread to see bedtime come. The dark of night only adds to the darkness of their minds and spirits. For people struggling with fear, darkness magnifies those fears.

The Word of God has some comforting things to say about nighttime. In Psalm 139 we're told God is with us everywhere and all the time, including in the dark of night (vv.7-11). We're also told the darkness is not dark to God, but to Him the night shines as the day so the darkness and the light are the same to Him (v.12, NRSV). In Psalm 121:3-4 we find God never sleeps. This Psalm also gives assurance that the Lord is our keeper both day and night and He will preserve us from evil. And best of all, He will preserve our souls (vv.5-7). The Psalmist knew God's keeping power and further states, "I will both lay me down in peace, and sleep: for thou, Lord, only makest me dwell in safety" (Psalm 4:8).

We don't have to be terrified in the night, because God covers us with His feathers and under His wings we can trust (Psalm 91:4). Can you picture a mother hen protecting her little chicks underneath her wings? That's the way God protects us in the night. Another helpful mental picture is God's love coming down upon us like a warm, cozy blanket. As we picture His love settling upon and around us, we can bask in that love and praise God for it. As small children, some of us were taught to repeat Isaiah 12:2 when we were fearful at night. "I will trust [God] and not be afraid" is still affirmation for us as adults.

PRAYER: O God, in these dark nights, I trust You are right here with me. Help me to remember Your presence is light around me.

Related verses: Psalm 63:5-6, 61:4; Psalm 91

PERFECT LOVE

"There is no fear in love, but perfect love casts out fear…" 1 John 4:18 (NRSV)

Some people see God only as a mean, stern dictator who is out to get them. Sometimes this perception of God is the one people have when they're in the wilderness. Because they don't feel God's love and presence, they become afraid of Him. And especially so if they never really felt His love for them prior to their wilderness experience. In 1 John 4 we're given some clues as to what the problem is. Verse 16 indicates we have to know and believe the love God has for us. We can *know* God's love to us because the Bible spells it out specifically. But do we *believe* it?

In order to *believe* God's love for us, we must exercise faith to believe in spite of what we feel. If we *believe* God's love, then we have no fear (are not afraid of God). What happens when our love is perfect and we aren't afraid of God? We're free to come boldly unto the throne of grace, that we may obtain mercy, and find grace to help in time of need (Hebrews 4:16). God wants us to come to Him with *all* of our thoughts, feelings, and problems. He wants us to believe he loves us so we're not afraid to express our anguish, hurts, and doubts to Him, even when those doubts are about Him. When we know and believe He loves us and are free to tell Him everything, then healing can begin and we start to find our way out of the wilderness.

PRAYER: O God, I choose to believe You love me even though I don't feel it right now. Since You *do* love me, I will tell You all about my hurts and problems.

Related verses: Ephesians 2:13, 3:12; 1 John 4:19

THE LORD UPHOLDS US

"The steps of a good man are ordered by the Lord: and he delighteth in his way. Though he fall, he shall not be utterly cast down: for the Lord upholdeth him with his hand." Psalm 37:23-24

The verses in Psalm 37:23-24 can be a comfort to us in our wilderness experiences. As far as we know, we are right with the Lord, so He is planning our steps. It's good to know God is delighting in our lives. What wonderful assurance to know that although we have "fallen" from our normal sense of well-being, God has promised we will not be totally cast down because He is holding us up with His hand. In those times when we're feeling low, that promise gives us hope.

It is reassuring to know that even though we can't sense God's presence, He is still in control of our lives and finds great pleasure in us. It gives us a sense of stability to know that although we are struggling in the wilderness, God is holding us up and won't let us go so far down that we will never be able to rise again and exit the wilderness.

In our wilderness experiences, we come to the place where we know our only hope for feeling better is to trust God, who is planning our lives and finding delight in us and who is holding us up with His hand. After all, if our all-powerful God can't bring us out of the wilderness, we sure can't bring ourselves out.

PRAYER: Thank You, God, that You uphold us when we're in the wilderness and You have the power to bring us out. Help me to trust You.

Related verses: Psalm 34:8, 63:8, 118:8-9, 145:14; Romans 4:20-21

INNER FATIGUE

"Wait on the Lord: be of good courage, and he shall strengthen thine heart..." Psalm 27:14

People in the wilderness know about fatigue—fatigue of body and mind. It can get so bad that we don't feel like doing anything. We may just want to sit or sleep. But God promises to strengthen our hearts if we wait on Him and take courage. The Lord, "the Creator of the ends of the earth" is able to do this for us because He Himself "fainteth not, neither is weary" (Isaiah 40:28). In verse 29 Isaiah says, "He giveth power to the faint; and to them that have no might he increaseth strength." Isaiah 25:4 tells us God has been a strength to the poor, a strength to the needy in their distress. People in the wilderness know what it's like to be a needy person in distress.

Isaiah 41:10 is a good verse to remember when we're experiencing inner fatigue and the problems associated with it: "Fear thou not; for I am with thee: be not dismayed; for I am thy God: I will strengthen thee...I will help thee...I will uphold thee with the right hand of my righteousness." If we repeat this verse over and over, and concentrate on its words, it helps us find hope in God. When we hope in God, He can strengthen our hearts (Psalm 31:24) and take care of our inner fatigue.

PRAYER: Thank You, God, for Your promise to strengthen us when we're feeling weak in spirit. Please strengthen my heart in this wilderness.

Related verses: Psalm 28:7, 29:11, 46:1, 73:26, 119:28, 138:3; Isaiah 12:2; Ephesians 3:16-17 (NRSV); 1 Peter 5:10

OVERWHELMED

"*C*ause me to hear thy lovingkindness in the morning; for in thee do I trust: cause me to know the way wherein I should walk; for I lift up my soul unto thee." Psalm 143:8

The cry of the Psalmist in Psalm 143 is the cry of our hearts when we're in a hard situation. Do these feelings sound familiar: life smitten down to the ground, dwelling in darkness (v.3)? Verse 4 further explains our feelings when we're in the wilderness: "Therefore is my spirit overwhelmed within me; my heart within me is desolate." Then the Psalmist tells what he does at these times. He meditates and muses on the works of God's hands (v.5). He also stretches forth his hands unto God and his soul thirsts for Him (v.6).

When we feel overwhelmed in the wilderness and thirst for God, do we lift up our souls to Him, and trust Him to bring us out of our trouble as the Psalmist did (vv.8, 11)? Do we ask God to teach us His will and lead us (v.10)? The Psalmist knew God's lovingkindness is better than life itself and affirmed, "my lips shall praise thee. Thus will I bless thee while I live: I will lift up my hands in thy name" (Psalm 63:3-4).

In the wilderness, we do well to follow the example of the Psalmist: "In the day of my trouble I call on [God], for [He] will answer me" (Psalm 86:7, NRSV).

PRAYER: O God, I feel just like the Psalmist did. Please help me in this time of trouble.

Related verses: Psalm 25:1, 34:15, 61:1-3, 86:4, 142:3a; Lamentations 3:41

GOD'S THOUGHTS TOWARD US

"*As* for me, I am poor and needy, but the Lord takes thought for me..." Psalm 40:17 (NRSV)

Do the words "poor and needy" describe how you're feeling today? Are you in the wilderness and feeling God has forgotten you? Take heart! The Word of God gives assurance that He *is* thinking about you.

Psalm 139:17-18 says, "How precious...are thy thoughts unto me, O God! how great is the sum of them! If I should count them, they are more in number than the sand..." Psalm 40:5 states: "Many, O Lord my God, are thy wonderful works which thou hast done, and thy thoughts which are [toward us]...they are more than can be numbered."

Perhaps in the wilderness you find it hard to believe God's thoughts toward you are good and He wants to do good things for you. In Jeremiah 29:11 (NRSV), God says, "For surely I know the plans I have for you, says the Lord, plans for your welfare and not for harm, to give you a future with hope."

Yes, even though you may be feeling poor and needy right now, be assured you are in God's thoughts and He has special plans for you.

PRAYER: Lord God, I *do* feel poor and needy. Thank You that you have me in your thoughts.

Related verses. Psalm 33:11, 139:1-5

WE'RE FREE!

"For the law of the Spirit of life in Christ Jesus hath made me free from the law of sin and death." Romans 8:2

We're free! The Bible says so! Because God sent His only Son, Jesus, to die for our sins, we are under grace (Romans 6:14). The magnitude of that truth is hard to grasp, but the only way to believe it—and to receive it—is by faith (Ephesians 2:8). Usually, we have little trouble believing and receiving the grace of God, but when we're in the wilderness, sometimes we begin to doubt. We begin to think, *I'm such a terrible person. I can't seem to live victoriously. I don't deserve the grace of God.*

None of us *deserves* the grace of God and that's exactly what makes it "grace." If we deserved it, we wouldn't need grace. No matter how hard we try to obey God and His Word, we'll never (in this life) attain perfection. Christ brought us liberty when He died for us and He doesn't want us to become "entangled again with the yoke of bondage" (Galatians 5:1).

God's grace is for us always—especially when we're in the wilderness. It's not what *we* do—but what *Jesus* did—that assures us of eternal life. Our part is to accept by faith God's grace and the freedom He gives. If Jesus makes us free, we are free indeed (John 8:36).

PRAYER: O God, thank You that freedom is for me right now in the wilderness. Help me, by faith, to accept Your wonderful grace.

Related verses: John 1:17; Romans 3:23-26, 6:18,22; 1 Peter 3:18

GOD'S NAME

"*And* they shall put my name upon the children of Israel; and I will bless them." Numbers 6:27

God told Moses to speak to the priests, Aaron and his sons, and tell them to bless the children of Israel (Numbers 6:22-26). Then they were to put God's name on the Israelites and God would bless them (v.27).

We are God's people also. We who trust in Him know His name (Psalm 9:10). There is power in His name and it is available to us just as it was to the Israelites (Psalm 20:7-8). When David faced the giant, Goliath, he told Goliath that he (David) was there "in the name of the Lord of hosts, the God of the armies of Israel" (1 Samuel 17:45).

The Psalmist knew the power of waiting on God's name (Psalm 52:9), and the power of calling upon His name when he was experiencing trouble and sorrow (Psalm 116:3-4). Proverbs 18:10 (NRSV) tells us "The name of the Lord is a strong tower; the righteous run into it and are safe."

When the Children of Israel were in the wilderness and later when they sinned by asking for a King, God said He would not forsake them for His great name's sake (1 Samuel 12:17,22). When *we* are in the wilderness—when we walk in darkness and have no light—the best thing we can do is "trust in the name of the Lord, and stay upon [our] God" (Isaiah 50:10).

PRAYER: Thank You, God, for Your great name. Help me to trust in Your name for strength and peace.

Related verses: Psalm 33:20-21, 124:8; Revelation 3:12

GOD'S WAY

"*L*ead me, O Lord, in thy righteousness…make thy way straight before my face." Psalm 5:8

We can get lost in the wilderness just as the Children of Israel did. And we begin to ask the same kinds of questions the Israelites asked: "Is God here or not? Can God do something for my situation? Where is the way?"

Like the Children of Israel in the wilderness, our minds are consumed with our daily needs and our situation. What we really need is more of God in our lives and a greater trust in Him. We're told in Psalm 37:5 (NRSV), to commit our way unto the Lord, trust in Him, and He will act. Yes, God is with us just as He was in the wilderness with the Children of Israel. Psalm 107:7 says, "And he led them forth by the right way…."

When we're in the wilderness and we feel as though we've lost the way, perhaps we need to give up our *own* way. If we're determined to go our own way, God cannot lead us in *His* way. God knows where we are and He wants us to turn to Him for guidance into *His* way. He promises He will instruct us and teach us in the way we should go, and He promises He will guide us with His eye (Psalm 32:8).

PRAYER: Lord God, help me to turn my eyes away from my circumstances and my own way and to trust You to lead me in *Your* way.

Related verses: Exodus 33:12-14; Psalm 25:12, 27:11, 37:34, 86:11

WEAK OR STRONG?

"... *W*hen I am weak, then am I strong." 2 Corinthians 12:10 What a paradox! How can we be strong if we are weak? Paul says in 2 Corinthians 12:9, "And [God] said unto me, My grace is sufficient for thee: for my strength is made perfect in weakness..." So it isn't *our* strength, but *God's* that produces power in us. It's the same strength David knew when he met the giant, Goliath. David told Goliath, "I come to thee in the name of the Lord of hosts" (1 Samuel 17:45). The Psalmist knew the strength of God and tells us to "Cast [our] burden upon the Lord, and he shall sustain [us]..." (Psalm 55:22).

We who are in the wilderness can know the same strength (God's) that Paul, David, and the Psalmist knew. Even though we feel weak, burdened, and inadequate, God promises to renew our strength if we wait upon Him (Isaiah 40:31). When we experience the grace of God and find out how much greater His strength is than our own, perhaps we'll be able to say as Paul said, "Most gladly therefore will I rather glory in my infirmities, that the power of Christ may rest upon me" (2 Corinthians 12:9). In the wilderness may we be able to declare: "The Lord is my strength and song, and is become my salvation" (Psalm 118:14).

PRAYER: O God, I feel so weak, so inadequate. Please be my strength and help me to experience Your sufficient grace.

Related verses: Psalm 18:1-2,32, 62:7, 71:16, 81:1, 105:4; Habakkuk 3:19

ESTABLISHED

"And after you have suffered for a little while, the God of all grace…will himself restore, support, strengthen, and establish you." 1 Peter 5:10 (NRSV)

When I was a young woman I met an older woman whom I greatly admired. Her calm, gentle nature and her understanding and care for others caught my attention. *What had happened in her life to make her such an outstanding person?* I wondered. Then I learned that earlier in her life she had a hard wilderness experience. And I noticed she continued to have hard things to deal with daily. But she exuded a peace and contentment that amazed me.

Now that I'm older and have gone through the wilderness myself, I understand what happens. It is the process Paul talks about in 1 Peter 5:10-11 (NRSV). After we have suffered awhile, God "will himself restore, support, strengthen, and establish" us. We come to a place of trusting the Lord when "evil tidings" come, and we're not afraid because our hearts are "established" (Psalm 112:7-8). We learn to "stay our minds" on God and trust Him, and God keeps us in perfect peace (Isaiah 26:3).

So take heart, you who are in the wilderness. You, too, will come to the place where you can say with the Psalmist, "O God, my heart is fixed; I will sing and give praise, even with thy glory" (Psalm 108:1).

PRAYER: Lord God, I long for You to restore, support, strengthen, and establish me. Please do Your work in me.

Related verses: Psalm 23:3, 27:1,5, 40:2; Proverbs 16:3

A PRESENT HELP

"*G*od is our refuge and strength, a very present help in trouble." Psalm 46:1

When we're in the wilderness, sometimes we get desperate to talk to someone. We feel we'll explode unless we can talk to someone *now*! But there's no one we can turn to. The people who support us aren't available.

Wait! There *is* Someone we can turn to. God is a very *present* help in trouble. He never goes on vacation, out to lunch, or on a business trip. He's right there this minute waiting for us to call on Him. He is our shelter, our place of safety from the turmoil of life. When we feel as though we've had it and we can't go on, He's our strength. And because God is our place of safety, our strength, and our help, we don't need to be afraid in this wilderness (Psalm 46:2-3).

We can pour out our troubles to God *right now* and He will minister to our spirits. He can help in a way no human being can.

PRAYER: God, You are my true refuge and strength. I pour out my troubles to You, believing You will help me. Thank You that You're always present.

Related verses: Psalm 4:3, 50:15, 86:7, 116:2, 145:18

BY GOD'S SPIRIT

"… *N*ot by might, nor by power, but by my Spirit, saith the Lord of hosts." Zechariah 4:6

What will it take to get us out of the wilderness? Do we think we have to exert our own power and influence? Do something drastic? Fight for our rights? Do we think someone else has to do something great for us? What can we depend on to exit the wilderness?

God says to us, "Be still, and know that I am God…" (Psalm 46:10). God wants us to turn our thoughts to Him, be quiet before Him and acknowledge that *He* is the One who can bring us through the wilderness. He says our coming out of the wilderness isn't going to be by any *person's* might or power, but only by His Spirit. God wants us to come to the place of relinquishment where we see the battle we're in as *God's* (2 Chronicles 20:15) and put our complete dependence on Him for deliverance. As long as we depend on our own ability to "pull ourselves up by our own bootstraps," we won't get far. But when we depend on God's Spirit to work for—and in—us, He will show us the way out.

PRAYER: Lord, help me to relinquish this wilderness experience to You and trust You to bring me through.

Related verses: Psalm 51:12; Isaiah 59:19; Joel 2:28-29; Matthew 10:20; Romans 8:11; Galatians 5:25; Ephesians 6:17

HOW LONG?

"*H*ow long must I bear pain in my soul, and have sorrow in my heart all day long?" Psalm 13:2 (NRSV)

"Pain in my soul" and "sorrow in my heart all day long" describe the feelings of people in the wilderness. Hard situations can go on and on, and we can struggle for years in the same situation. In these situations we often feel like the Psalmist when he said, "How long wilt thou forget me, O Lord? Forever? How long wilt thou hide thy face from me?" (Psalm 13:1). But even though we often feel God has rejected us, God is our only hope (Psalm 62:5, NRSV). He promises to answer us when we call upon Him, and to be with us in trouble (Psalm 91:15). In our hard times, God wants to be our refuge and strength and our "very present help in trouble" (Psalm 46:1).

What do we desire when we're in the wilderness? To escape from our situation? To be able to endure the wilderness and come out on the other side? God may not want us to leave our hard situation and He may not change the circumstances in it, but He will be faithful to His promises to be our salvation in the wilderness, to always be with us even when we doubt His presence, and to remain as our refuge and strength and help. When our desires honor God, He will fulfill them in His timing (Psalm 145:19).

PRAYER: O God, I have pain in my soul and sorrow in my heart. But You promise to deliver me. Help me to wait for Your timing.

Related verses: Psalm 22:11, 27:9; Psalm 62:1-8; John 14:18

DEPENDENT UPON GOD

"*A*s the eyes of servants look to the hand of their master, as the eyes of a maid to the hand of her mistress, so our eyes look to the Lord our God, until he has mercy upon us." Psalm 123:2 (NRSV)

How dependent are we upon God? When all is going well in our lives, we tend to feel self-sufficient. But then a hard situation comes along and we find ourselves in the wilderness. We begin to see that of ourselves we won't make it. Do we then turn our eyes to God and wait on Him to have mercy on us in the same way the servant looks "to the hand of their master" and "the maid to the hand of her mistress?"

In Bible times, a servant and maid were totally dependent on their master and mistress, not only for daily sustenance but also for instruction and guidance. Life for them was centered on the will of their owners and they waited on them with expectancy. That kind of dependency is what we need to have on God, especially when we're in the wilderness. God will provide the grace, strength, and peace we need each day. He will instruct and guide us. When we center our lives upon God's will and turn our eyes upon the Lord our God and wait with expectancy (hope), He will have mercy on us.

PRAYER: Lord God, I'm so dependent on You. Help me to keep my eyes upon You as I wait for Your mercy.

Related verses: Psalm 25:10, 33:18-22, 46:1, 123:1; Isaiah 26:3; 2 Corinthians 12:9

INTO PEACE

"*B*y the tender mercy of our God, the dawn from on high will break upon us, to give light to those who sit in darkness and in the shadow of death, to guide our feet into the way of peace." Luke 1:78-79, NRSV

These verses in Luke explain what Jesus does for those who are in the darkness of sin and close to spiritual death. But the words, "who sit in darkness and in the shadow of death" also describe how we can feel when we're in the wilderness. We feel we are in darkness. We think we'll never feel any better. Our situation seems entirely hopeless. In fact, everything seems so hopeless that sometimes we would welcome death.

Just as Jesus came to bring peace to the sinner, so He came to guide the feet of the person in emotional darkness into the way of peace. Jesus said, "Peace I leave with you, my peace I give unto you..." (John 14:27).

Jesus doesn't *zap* us and all of a sudden we have peace. Luke 1:78-79 says He will guide us *into* the way of peace. It's a process. And when we're suffering emotionally, it usually takes more time than we think it should. But we have to trust ourselves to *God's* way and let Him guide us. The way He chooses to guide us into peace will be the right way for our particular situation. God may not change our situation or circumstances, but in His timing He *will* bring us into the way of peace. And He can do this while we're in the wilderness.

PRAYER: Jesus, everything feels so dark and hopeless. You are my only hope. Please shine on me and guide me into peace. Help me to trust Your way and timing.

Related verses: John 16:33; Philippians 4:6-7 (NRSV)

TRUTH

"*Lead me in thy truth, and teach me…*" Psalm 25:5

In the wilderness it's easy to get caught up in believing untruth. There is much that is not truth in the world and it's hard to know what is truth and what isn't because it all sounds so right and good. Even so-called "good" books sometimes carry untruths. One such book says love is a *feeling* and if you don't *feel* love, it isn't real love. Nowhere in God's Word do we love is based on feelings. Real love as given in 1 Corinthians 13 is based on action and never ends (v.8, NRSV). We have to be discerning of what we read, what we hear, and what we see.

How will we know what is truth and what isn't? John 16:13 tells us the Holy Spirit guides us into all truth. If we let the Holy Spirit have control of our life, He will enlighten us to truth and error. The Word of God is truth (John 17:17) and guides us in knowing what is truth. The Psalmist desired that God's light and truth would lead him (Psalm 43:3).

Jesus said, "I am the way, the truth and the life…" (John 14:6). As followers of Jesus, we can know what is truth. We need not believe things that aren't true when we're in the wilderness.

PRAYER: O God, there's so much that sounds good and right and true. Lead me by Your Holy Spirit to discern what is truth and what is error.

Related verses: Psalm 25:10, 86:11,15, 91:4, 119:30, 146:5-6; 1 John 4:6

GOD IS ABLE

"For [God has] been a strength to the poor, a strength to the needy in [their] distress, a refuge from the storm, a shadow from the heat…" Isaiah 25:4

Our God can meet any of our needs. He is able to be a strength to us when we're poor—even when we're poor emotionally for whatever reason.

When we're in the wilderness, we experience much distress. God can be our strength in any kind of distress. We feel the storm of negative feelings, the storm of temptations to worry and fret, and the storm of conflict. God is able to be our refuge in the storm. God is able to be as a shadow from the heat, like the coolness we feel on a hot day when we walk from the sunshine into the shadow of a tree or building. The heat in the wilderness can seem unbearable at times, but when we go to God, He can provide the "shade" we need.

What is it in the wilderness that is causing you to feel poor and needy? That seems like a storm, or "puts the heat on"? God is able to be your coolness, your refuge, and your strength.

PRAYER: Tell God about your problems, your feelings, and your needs. Ask Him to be your strength, refuge, and your cool shadow.

Related verses: Psalm 46:1, Daniel 3:17; Matthew 9:28; Romans 4:20-21; 2 Corinthians 9:8; Ephesians 3:20-21; 2 Timothy 1:12; Hebrews 2:18; Jude 24-25

PROMISES FOR TODAY

"Fear thou not; for I am with thee: be not dismayed; for I am thy God: I will strengthen thee; yea, I will help thee; yea, I will uphold thee with the right hand of my righteousness." Isaiah 41:10

God's Word contains many promises that can help us when we're in the wilderness. Often God will direct us to certain promises we know are just for us on a particular day. One of the great verses of promise is Isaiah 41:10. The promises in this verse cover just about any kind of hard situation in which we find ourselves.

Are we fearful and afraid? God tells us we needn't fear because He is with us. Are we discouraged? God says we aren't to be dismayed because He is our God. Do we feel weak and unable to bear the burdens of the wilderness? God says, "I will strengthen you." Do we lack direction and aren't able to make necessary decisions? God assures us that He will help us. Do we feel we might not make it through this wilderness? God says, "I will uphold you with my victorious right hand" (NRSV).

In Isaiah 41:10, and in many other verses, God assures us that He knows all about our situation and will be all we need, if we let Him. It's good to write down the promises of God and have them on hand for those times when we feel overwhelmed with the impossibility of our situation.

PRAYER: Thank You, God, for who You are, and for Your promises for me today. Enable me to believe them and to depend on You to make them real in my life.

Related verses: 1 Kings 8:56; 2 Corinthians 1:20; 2 Peter 1:3-4

FLY AWAY?

"... *O*that I had wings like a dove! for then would I fly away and be at rest. I would hasten my escape from the windy storm and tempest." Psalm 55:6,8

Do the words of the Psalmist express your longings right now? *I've had it! I just want to get away from this hard situation."*

When we're in the wilderness, we sometimes have the same feelings the Psalmist expressed. We wish we had wings like a bird so we could fly away from our troubles and have peace of mind. We want to escape from the "storm and tempest" in our lives. When things get really bad, we may even want to go on to heaven. The Apostle Paul felt that way sometimes too (2 Corinthians 5:4).

As long as we're in this life, escape is not the answer. True, we might get away from the situation or people who are causing our troubles, but that wouldn't take care of the work that needs to go on *within* us. Those lessons of patience, unconditional love, trust, and whatever else we need to learn would still be waiting for us. Hebrews 12:1 tells us to "run with patience the race that is set before us." We're also told to endure hardness as a good soldier of Jesus Christ (2 Timothy 2:3). It's a normal feeling to long to fly away (escape) when we're in the wilderness, but we need to determine to hang in there for the long haul. Jesus tells us, "he that endureth to the end shall be saved" (Matthew 10:22).

PRAYER: O God, the way is so hard and I long to escape. Help me to endure and to learn the lessons You have for me.

Related verses: Psalm 6:2-4, 55:4-6; Hebrews 10:36

OUR SHEPHERD

"The Lord is my Shepherd, I shall not want." Psalm 23:1

Jesus understands and sympathizes with the feelings of grief, anguish, fear, disappointment and despair that hound us in the wilderness. When He was here on earth He showed His understanding and care for the feelings of those around Him. Jesus said, "...I have compassion on the multitude, because they continue with me now three days, and have nothing to eat: and I will not send them away fasting, lest they faint in the way" (Matthew 15:32). Isaiah 40:11 describes our compassionate Shepherd: "He shall feed his flock like a shepherd: he shall gather the lambs with his arm, and carry them in his bosom, and shall gently lead those that are with young."

Jesus understands our feelings in the wilderness, but He doesn't desire that we wallow in those feelings. He encourages us to "Fear not, little flock; for it is your Father's good pleasure to give you the kingdom" (Luke 12:32). Jesus is also able to change our feelings. He invites those who are in the wilderness to "Come unto me, all ye that labor and are heavy laden, and I will give you rest" (Matthew 11:28). He will give rest unto our souls (v.29). Jesus is our compassionate Shepherd who leads us beside the *still* waters and restores our souls (Psalm 23:2-3).

PRAYER: Thank You, Jesus, that You are my loving Shepherd. Please give me Your rest.

Related verses: Psalm 78:52; John 10:11,14-15,27,28; Hebrews 13:20-21; 1 Peter 5:4

WATER IN THE WILDERNESS

"...I GIVE *WATER IN THE WILDERNESS,*
RIVERS IN THE DESERT,
TO GIVE DRINK TO MY CHOSEN PEOPLE,
THE PEOPLE WHOM I FORMED FOR MYSELF
SO THAT THEY MIGHT DECLARE MY PRAISE."
ISAIAH 43:20-21 (NRSV)

THIRSTY

"*I* will open rivers on the bare heights, and fountains in the midst of the valleys; I will make the wilderness a pool of water, and the dry land springs of water." Isaiah 41:18 (NRSV)

As the Children of Israel traveled through the wilderness, sometimes they couldn't find water. Then they would cry out against Moses, their leader. When Moses went before God with the problem, God supplied water for His people (Exodus 17:1-6). Along with the water, He gave them a new understanding of who He was and what He could do for them.

We, too, become thirsty in the wilderness. We long to know why we're there and what we can do to get out. When we get thirsty enough, we finally come to the place where we're ready to seek God and let Him satisfy our thirst in *His* way. When we take our eyes off our hard situation and seek God's way in the wilderness, He begins to give us insights and understanding that will hasten our exit from the wilderness.

As we open our minds to God's teaching, His refining and purifying become as refreshing and renewing water to our thirsty souls. We finally see change within ourselves and we welcome it as a way to growth and maturity. We know these waters of understanding and renewal aren't just for the wilderness, but will benefit us the rest of our lives. As He did with the Children of Israel, God brings forth water when we're in the wilderness to humble us and to prove us—to do us good in the end (Deuteronomy 8:15-16, NRSV).

PRAYER: Help me, Lord, to open my heart to Your waters of understanding and renewal. I desire to grow and mature in the wilderness.

Related verses: Psalm 63:1, 107:35; Isaiah 35:6, 41:17-18; John 4:14, 7:37-39

GROWING

"… We must go through many hardships to enter the kingdom of God." Acts 14:22 (NIV)

Just as loving parents desire to see their children grow and mature, so God loves us so much that He wants us—His children—to grow and mature. This growing involves a special refining, and lessons God knows we need to learn. But He doesn't leave us to "go it" alone in the process. God is right with us watching that the refining fire doesn't get too hot or too cold (Malachi 3:3).

In order for us to grow and mature, God has to allow tribulation in our lives (Romans 5:3-5). He doesn't, however, close His eyes to our hard times, but is merciful and comforts us in all our troubles (2 Corinthians 1:3-4). Because God loves us, He chastens and corrects us when we need it (Proverbs 3:11-12, Hebrews 12:6-13, Revelation 3:19). He does this for our good, so we can share in His holiness (Hebrews 12:10, NIV).

In order for our faith to be strengthened, God allows it to be tried through temptations so it will be found unto praise and honor and glory when Jesus comes (1 Peter 1:6-7). God promises we will not be tempted too much, but He will make a way of escape so we'll be able to bear it (1 Corinthians 10:13).

God, our loving Heavenly Father, knows just what we need every day of our lives. He doesn't willingly afflict or grieve us (Lamentations 3:33) but allows those hardships that are for our good and prepare us for heaven (Acts 14:22).

PRAYER: Father God, thank You for Your great love that cares about every aspect of my growing and maturing. Help me to trust You to carry out that process in the way You know is best. Amen.

Related verses: Deuteronomy 7:8-9; Psalm 69:16-17; 2 Thessalonians 1:3-41 John 3:1, 4:16

JESUS' KEEPING POWER

"... *I* know whom I have believed, and am persuaded that he is able to keep that which I have committed unto him against that day." 2 Timothy 1:12

Normally, it's somewhat scary not knowing the future, but it's *really* scary not knowing the future when we're in the wilderness. What changes will occur in the world, in my country, in my state, in my area, in my own personal life that will require me to remain true to my family, my friends, my church, but most of all, to God? Will I be able to stand firm, to remain faithful to God's truth?

If it all depended on me, I would be too frightened to go on living, because I know my own limitations—my own weaknesses. But because I have believed Jesus and have committed my life, my future—everything—to Him, I need not be afraid. And because I have seen His working in my life in times past, I am persuaded (convinced, sure) that Jesus is able to keep me—and all that concerns me—true to Himself till I see Him face to face. It's because of Jesus' ability to keep what we have committed to Him that we can face the future and rest in peace each day.

PRAYER: Lord Jesus, thank You that we can know You and have the assurance of Your keeping power of all we commit to You.

Related verses: Psalm 37:5; Proverbs 16:3; Acts 20:32; Colossians 1:12-14; 2 Timothy 4:18

LOOKING AHEAD

"... *T*his one thing I do, forgetting those things which are behind, and reaching forth unto those things which are before, I press toward the mark for the prize of the high calling of God in Christ Jesus." Philippians 3:13-14

Are there things in the past that continue to hold you in the wilderness? If so, the Apostle Paul's example of "forgetting those things which are behind" is for you. What things in the past does God want you to forget?

Were there times when you didn't follow God's way? Maybe the regrets keep coming back to haunt you even though you've asked for God's forgiveness. 1 John 1:9 assures us that if we confess our sins, God is faithful to forgive our sins. God blots out our sins and remembers them no more (Isaiah 43:25).

Have other people hurt you or failed to live up to your expectations? Even though they may not have done so intentionally, are you still hugging those hurts and failures to your heart? Can you forgive others as you want God to forgive you (Matthew 6:14)? Perhaps you have failed to live up to your own expectations of yourself. Are you able to forgive yourself? Jesus wants us to lay the "if onlys" at His feet and leave them there.

What else in your past needs to be forgotten so you are free to focus on "those things which are before" and free to "press toward the mark for the prize of the high calling of God in Christ Jesus?"

PRAYER: Lord God, enable me to give to You—and then forget—the past hurts and mistakes which keep me from pressing onward as Your person.

Related verses: Isaiah 44:22; 2 Corinthians 5:17; Philippians 1:6; 2 Timothy 1:12

WAIT PATIENTLY

"*I* waited patiently for the Lord; and he [listened to] me, and heard my cry. He brought me up also out of an horrible pit, out of the miry clay, and set my feet upon a rock, and established my goings." Psalm 40:1-2

There were times in my life when I felt low, depressed—as if I were in "an horrible pit" and in "the miry clay." I felt as though I would never get out of the wilderness and enjoy life again. I became desperate for a way out. But with all my efforts and all my struggling, I wasn't able to make myself feel differently.

After going through a number of these episodes, I began to see that God had *His* way and *His* timing for my deliverance. There were lessons He wanted me to learn in the process of feeling better. It was only when I began to "wait patiently" for Him to do the healing, that I could have hope of His bringing me to a better place. When I truly relinquished my situation and my desperation to Him and left them with Him, He "listened and heard my cry." Each time He would indeed bring me "up out of an horrible pit, set my feet upon a rock and establish my goings" ("making my steps secure" (NRSV). But always in His way and in His timing.

God wants to make a way for you in the wilderness. And He will, when you trust Him enough to give Him your situation and your desperation, *leave them with Him*, and wait patiently for His deliverance.

PRAYER: Lord God, help me to trust my situation and my desperate feelings to You. Help me to wait patiently for Your way through the wilderness.

Related verses: Psalm 25:5, 27:14, 37:7, 62:5; Isaiah30:18, 40:31; Lamentations 3:25-26

PRAYER

"*P*ray without ceasing." 1 Thessalonians 5:17

Prayer is talking to God and listening for Him to speak. But when we're in the wilderness it's sometimes hard to pray, and for some people, impossible. God seems so far away. Our prayers seem to go no higher than the ceiling. We wonder if God even hears us. And yet, praying is one of the most therapeutic things we can do when we're feeling "down." Many times, God is the only one around to talk to.

In the wilderness I find it helpful simply to say: *God, my prayers seem to be going no higher than the ceiling. I don't know if You're hearing me, but I'm going to talk to You anyway.* Then I proceed to talk to Him about my hard situation, my low and desperate feelings, and my hurts and disappointments. It helps! I have often been surprised at how much better it makes me feel.

There have been times when I thought: *God knows all about my situation and how I feel, so why tell Him again?* It wasn't until I actually took the time to talk to Him about my situation and feelings—again—that I felt a difference in my spirit, received assurance, or felt a ray of hope.

It really is good advice to "pray without ceasing" (talk to God continually) when we're in the wilderness. He assures us He *does* hear and will answer (Psalm 91:15).

PRAYER: Oh God, You seem so far away. But You say You hear me, so I'm going to talk to You right now. (Tell Him your problems, how you feel, and your need of Him).

Related verses: Psalm 141:1-2, 4:1, 5:1-3, 6:9, 38:15, 50:15, 55:17, 116:1-2; Proverbs 15:8

PERFECT PEACE

"*T*hou wilt keep [those] in perfect peace, whose mind is stayed on thee: because [they trust] in thee." Isaiah 26:3

When we're in the wilderness, negative thoughts go round and round, replaying in our minds. It takes concentration and brute effort to keep giving those thoughts to God and turning our minds to the positive.

What is the key to having peace in difficult situations? We see in Isaiah 26:3, the bottom line is trusting God. And if we truly trust God, our minds will be stayed on Him. "Stayed" in the sense of having Him in our thoughts constantly instead of letting our minds dwell on ourselves and our difficulties. And "stayed" also in the sense we trust God so completely that our faith is anchored in Him, and we are totally assured of who God is and what He can do for us. When we come to that place, God not only gives us peace, He can *keep* us in perfect peace. But we have to do our part in order for God to do His. We have to trust God and stay (fix) our minds on Him.

PRAYER: O God, help me to have that deep trust in You which enables me to stay my mind on You. Thank You that You're able to keep me in perfect peace, even in hard situations.

Related verses: Psalm 4:8, 29:11, 55:22, 85:8, 119:165; Proverbs 3:1-2; Isaiah 12:2, 55:12; Luke 24:36; John 14:27, 20:19,21,26; Romans 8:6; Philippians 4:6-7; 2 Thessalonians 3:16

STRENGTH IN WEAKNESS

"... *My* grace is sufficient for thee: for my strength is made perfect in weakness..." 2 Corinthians 12:9

"Weakness." No one likes that word. We don't want to be weak. But we do feel weak at times, especially in the wilderness. We struggle to be strong. To be in control. To be self-sufficient. To be on top of everything. And yet 2 Corinthians 12:9 indicates that weakness isn't all bad.

As long as by ourselves we're able to be strong, in control, self-sufficient, and on top of everything, we don't need God. We don't experience His grace and strength. It's in our weakness that we can know God's strength and grace. So the Apostle Paul says, "Most gladly therefore will I rather glory in my infirmities, that the power of Christ may rest upon me. Therefore I take pleasure in infirmities…for when I am weak, then am I strong" (vv.9-10).

What is Paul saying? He's saying it's actually best to be weak in ourselves. To *not* be in control or self-sufficient and on top of everything in our own strength. He's saying *God's power* is where it's at. It's when we're weak and let God's power come through that we're truly strong.

Let's not feel down on ourselves for being weak, but accept our weakness as an opportunity for God's power to rest upon us. Then we'll know true strength.

PRAYER: Help me, God, to accept my weakness and to let Your grace be sufficient, as Your strength is made perfect in me.

Related verses: Psalm 61:2-3; Isaiah 35:3-4; Matthew 28:18; 1 Corinthians 1:27; 2 Corinthians 4:7; Ephesians 3:20-21, 6:10; Colossians 1:11

CAST BURDENS UPON THE LORD

"*C*ast thy burden upon the Lord, and he shall sustain thee..." Psalm 55:22

The idea of "casting" our burden upon the Lord is intriguing. We find this concept again in 1 Peter 5:7: "Casting all your care upon him; for he careth for you."

Why didn't these writers simply say, "Put" your burden upon the Lord or "giving" all your cares to Him? Often when we have burdens or cares, that's exactly what we do. We put our burden upon the Lord or give our cares to Him, but instead of continuing to let Him have them, we take them back and again try to handle them ourselves.

The "casting" in these scriptures indicates a *throwing* of our burdens and cares upon God and then leaving them there instead of half-heartedly giving them to Him and then taking them back again. We must determine to let Him have them. The Psalmist indicates it's only when we do cast our burdens upon God in the sense of leaving them there, that God will sustain us.

PRAYER: Help me, God, to *throw* my burdens and cares upon You and then leave them there.

Related verses: Psalm 3:5, 37:5; Matthew 6:25,33, 11:28-30; Philippians 4:6-7

WAKEFUL NIGHT HOURS

"My soul is satisfied as with a rich feast, and my mouth praises you with joyful lips when I think of you on my bed, and meditate on you in the watches of the night." Psalm 63:5-6 (NRSV)

Nights can be long in the wilderness. Our problems seem worse in the stillness and darkness of night. Worries and fears crowd in and sleep eludes us. But these awake times need not be wasted.

The Psalmist knew how to make the most of his sleepless times. He says when he's in bed and thinks of God and meditates on Him in the night, his soul is satisfied and his mouth praises God with joyful lips.

We, too, can choose what we do with our wakeful night hours. We can worry and think negative thoughts and thus drive sleep further from us. Or we can choose to meditate on God and praise Him, which helps our body relax and allows sleep to come more easily. We may find we fall back to sleep much more quickly if we give our worries and fears to God and thank Him that He's working out our problems. It also helps to pray for others, or simply repeat the name of Jesus while we focus our mind on Him.

PRAYER: Lord God, in those times when I can't sleep, help me to give You my fears and worries and then spend my time in communion with You.

Related verses: Psalm 139:12, 42:8; Proverbs 3:24; Luke 6:12

GOD, OUR FATHER

"...*J*esus...lifted up his eyes to heaven, and said, Father...Holy Father...O righteous Father." John 17:1,11,25

Jesus, our perfect example, always addressed God as "Father." True, Jesus was God's *Son*. But in John 20:17, Jesus tells Mary to go to his brothers and say to them, "I ascend unto my Father and *your* Father" (meaning *our* Father also). In The Sermon on the Mount alone (Matthew 5,6,7) Jesus says "*your* Father" at least ten times.

Romans 8:15-16 tells us we have been adopted by God as His children. So we are His sons and daughters and "joint-heirs with Christ" (v.17). Isaiah 63:16 says doubtless God is our Father. What must it do to the Father heart of God if His children can't—or won't—accept Him as their Father? In Galatians 4:6 we're told that because we're sons (and daughters) of God, He has put the Spirit of Jesus into our hearts, crying, Abba, Father. So if we have the Spirit of Jesus in us, we will be able to call God "Father."

Perhaps some of us find it hard to think of God as "Father" because our earthly fathers failed or rejected us. If so, let's imagine in our minds what a *perfect* father would be like. Is he one who would spend time with us? Would never let us down? Would love us unconditionally? Would always be there for us?

God is that kind of Father—and much more. If we study the Word, we will see what a wonderful Father God is to us. Then when that realization grips our minds and hearts, we can begin to know God as "Father."

PRAYER: Thank You, God, that You are our loving heavenly Father. Help me to receive Your Father love.

Related verses: Psalm 27:10, 68:5, 89:26; Isaiah 64:8; Matthew 6:8,9, 7:11, 10:29; Romans 1:7; 1 Corinthians 8:6; Ephesians 4:6

REMEMBER GOD'S WORKS

"*I* will remember the works of the Lord: surely I will remember thy wonders of old." Psalm 77:11

"Why doesn't God do something?" we ask in the wilderness. "This hard time goes on and on."

In Psalm 77 we're given a helpful and encouraging exercise for our situation, and that is to remember how God has worked in our lives—and in the lives of others—in the past. The Psalmist was in trouble. His spirit was overwhelmed. He couldn't sleep (vv.1-4). He was tempted to distrust God (vv.7-9). Then in verse 10 he says, "This is my infirmity: but I will remember the years of the right hand of the most High" (the years when I could see God working in my life). The Psalmist decided he would meditate on God's works and think about God's doings (v.12). And he asks a profound question: "Who is so great a God as our God?" Then he makes this statement of confidence to God: "Thou art the God that doest wonders" (vv.13-14). After that affirmation, the Psalmist continues to remember—and to tell about— the works of God.

What has God done for you or for other people you know? And what about all the wonderful things you read about God doing in the Bible? Or even the wonders of God in creation—the beauty and awesomeness all around you?

Remembering the works and wonders of God in the past gives hope for His working in our lives now and in the future.

PRAYER: Creator God, thank You for all the wonderful things You have done in the past. I believe You will continue to do wonders in my life now, and in the days to come.

Related verses: Exodus 15:11; Psalm 40:5, 73:28, 86:8, 92:5, 104:24, 105:1-5, 107:1-31, 111:4, 139:14, 143:5; Psalm 145; Daniel 4:3; Acts 15:12

NEW FOCUS

"*S*ing unto the Lord a new song, and his praise from the end of the earth..." Isaiah 42:10

What is the focus of our thoughts and prayers in the wilderness? Do we think only of ourselves and our situation and neglect to give God praise? Are our prayers full of complaints and "gimmes"? Do we attend church only for the social time it provides and not for the opportunity to worship God along with other Christians? In my life during the week, do I lament the drudgery of each day and see only the negatives of my surroundings and the world at large?

If we answered these questions with a "yes," it will require a change in our focus if we want to find the way out of the wilderness.

Right now, we can resolve to change the focus of our prayers and spend time praising God. We can decide we'll turn our thoughts to God when we're in His house. We can resolve to look for the positive and learn to dwell on the good in the world. We can determine to develop an attitude of thankfulness for our everyday blessings in spite of the hard things.

It's amazing what praising God and learning gratefulness can do for us when we're in the wilderness. Perhaps in a few days or weeks, we'll be able to say with the Psalmist: "And he hath put a new song in my mouth, even praise unto our God" (Psalm 40:3).

PRAYER: I need a new focus in my thoughts and prayers, Lord. Help me to develop a spirit of gratitude, and praise You with my words and actions every day of the week.

Related verses: 1Chronicles 29:10-13; Psalm 69:30, 71:8, 75:1, Psalm 100, 105:1, 106:1; 107:21-22, 116:17, 149:1

IMPORTANCE OF WORDS

"*S*et a watch, O Lord, before my mouth; keep the door of my lips." Psalm 141:3

Because of our negative feelings when we're in the wilderness, it's hard to keep our words positive. Why are the words we speak so important?

By our words our negative feelings have a way of spilling over into our relationships with those around us and causing much hurt. It's especially hard not to take out our feelings on our spouse, children, and others close to us.

When we're feeling low, it's important we resolve within ourselves not to harm others by our words. We can't control our tongues by ourselves, however. James 3:8-10 says none of us can tame our tongue and out of the same mouth comes good and bad. James also says this shouldn't be. That's why it's necessary we pray the Psalmist's prayer: "Set a watch, O Lord, before my mouth; keep the door of my lips." When we depend on God, He will help us speak positive and loving words when we're feeling low. The more we let God rule our life, the more He'll be able to control our tongue.

PRAYER: Lord, I want to speak only positive and helpful words. Guard my lips so every word I speak will be what You want me to say.

Related verses: Psalm 35:28, 39:1; Proverbs 8:6-7; Matthew 15:10-11; Colossians 3:8-10; James 1:19; 1 Peter 3:10

TELL JESUS EVERYTHING

"And the apostles gathered themselves together unto Jesus, and told him all things, both what they had done, and what they had taught." Mark 6:30

Can you see in your mind's eye that motley group of apostles excitedly telling Jesus about what had happened—how they had carried out the work He had called them to do and taught the life-giving words He had instructed them to teach? It was apparent the apostles felt a special closeness to Jesus, and His acceptance of them gave them the freedom to share "all" with Him.

It's hard not to envy the apostles' relationship with Jesus. And yet, even though Jesus isn't here in person today, through His Spirit we, too, can be close to Him. We can tell Him all we do and how we feel—when we're happy or when we're lonely and sad and in the wilderness. He is right with us and in us and waiting for us to talk to Him. Sometimes we think: *Jesus knows how I feel anyway, so why tell Him?* But it's when we stop and actually talk to Him about our situation and feelings that it makes a difference in our lives. We can have the same close relationship with Jesus that the apostles had.

PRAYER: Lord Jesus, thank You that You accept me as you did the apostles. I want to tell You everything and experience that closeness with You.

Related verses: Exodus 33:11a; John 15:14-15; Philippians 4:6-7

GOD'S DWELLING PLACE

"For thus saith the high and lofty One that inhabiteth eternity, whose name is Holy; I dwell in the high and holy place, with him also that is of a contrite and humble spirit, to revive the spirit of the humble, and to revive the heart of the contrite ones." Isaiah 57:15

Isn't it wonderful that our God—the high and Holy God who dwells in the high and holy place (Heaven)—is also willing, and even wants, to dwell with mere humans? There seems to be a condition, however, for God to dwell with us, and the condition is that we have a contrite and humble spirit.

Our pride in thinking we can work out our own problems can lead us into the wilderness. But sooner or later we experience contriteness and humility. We come to realize we can't change our situation nor the people in it. There is nothing we can do. We finally see we are totally dependent on God. When we get to that place and recognize *we* can't change *anything*, including our feelings, and ourselves God can work in us. He says His dwelling place is with us in our contriteness and humbleness and He will revive our spirits and our hearts. Let's take hope in that promise.

PRAYER: God, I give this situation and myself to You. There's nothing I can do. Please revive my heart and spirit.

Related verses: 2 Chronicles 34:27; Job 22:29; Psalm 34:18, 51:17; Proverbs 16:19; Isaiah 66:1-2; Matthew 5:3,5; Colossians 3:12; James 4:6

FRUIT BEARERS

"Every branch that bears fruit he prunes to make it bear more fruit." John 15:2

We have grapevines in our back yard and every year my husband cuts back the branches, including those branches that yielded grapes the year before. He cuts them *way* back. To a person who doesn't understand about grapevines, it doesn't seem to make sense to prune those branches that were so fruitful the year before. I, myself, look at those poor, cut-back branches and wonder how they can ever produce more grapes. But if they weren't pruned, they would bear very few grapes another year and the grapes they *would* bear, would be of poor quality. Let go, those branches would soon stop bearing altogether.

Jesus indicates that's the way it is with us. In John 15, He says He is the vine and we are the branches (v.5). His Father (God) is the husbandman (vine dresser-v.1). If we bear fruit, God purges (or prunes) us so we will bear *more* fruit. If He wouldn't prune us, we would gradually stop bearing fruit altogether. If life were all "roses"— everything nice and easy—it's likely we would become so engrossed in ourselves that we would forget about working for God. God's pruning keeps us aware that bearing fruit for Him is what we were created to do.

PRAYER: Thank You, Father, that You know what we need in order to remain fruit bearers. We trust You, our Master Pruner.

Related verses: Malachi 3:2-3; John 15:8; Romans 5:3-5; Hebrews 12:7-13

GOD'S WORD AGAINST SATAN

"[God] only is my rock and my salvation: he is my defense; I shall not be moved." Psalm 62:6

There seem to be times in our lives when we're more vulnerable to wilderness experiences. Satan knows our weaknesses and he comes to us with temptations or negative thoughts, self-pity, low self-esteem, and many other things that contribute to depression and despair.

James 4:7 tells us to "Resist the devil, and he will flee from you." When Jesus was tempted by Satan in the wilderness, Jesus used the Word of God to resist Satan. So when Satan comes to us with temptations, we too, can use God's Word against him. One good verse to use is Psalm 62:6. We can tell Satan, "Get out of here and let me alone. God is my rock. He is my defence. I shall not be moved by you." Then we can picture ourselves in a cleft (crack) of the rock (God) with God's hand over us to protect us from Satan. When we resist Satan in this way, he will flee.

Each one of us has different kinds of temptations and when we go to God, He will show us how to use His Word to resist Satan. God is indeed our rock, our salvation, and our defence, and we can say, "I shall not be moved."

PRAYER: O God, show me how to resist Satan when he tempts me. Thank You that You are my rock, my salvation, and my defense.

Related verses: Matthew 4:10-11, 26:41; Ephesians 6:10-18; 1 Peter 5:8-9

SACRIFICE OF PRAISE

"By him therefore let us offer the sacrifice of praise to God continually, that is, the fruit of our lips giving thanks to his name." Hebrews 13:15

When life is going well, we feel like praising God. But when life is hard—in the wilderness—praising God is not the natural thing to do. We really don't *feel* like praising Him.

Hebrews 13:5 says we are to offer the "sacrifice" of praise to God *continually* (all the time). That means when we feel like it—and when we don't. Our feelings—high or low—don't change God. They don't change the fact that He is *always* worthy of our praise. Do we thank God for who He is and what He has done for us? Or do our praises depend on our feelings at the moment and what we think God *should be* doing?

When we don't feel thankful or feel like praising God, it does take a sacrifice on our part to praise Him anyway. In those times we can tell God: *I don't feel like praising, but I know You are always worthy to be praised, so I offer praise as my sacrifice to You.* Then we can praise and thank God for who He is and even for our wilderness experience (Ephesians 5:20) because *I know You have some purpose for allowing it, God.*

PRAYER: Lord God, teach me how to offer the sacrifice of praise to You—and to do it continually, even when I don't feel like it.

Related verses: Psalm 34:1, 92:1-2, 116:17, 145:1-2; Psalm 150

TAKING UP OUR CROSS

"[*J*esus said], If any man will come after me, let him deny himself, and take up his cross, and follow me. For whosoever will save his life shall lose it: and whosoever will lose his life for my sake shall find it." Matthew 16:24-25

We don't hear much about denying ourselves. It seems "me-ism" is the religion of the day. *I* have to satisfy *me*. *I* have to have what *I* want right now. *I* have to be on top. *I* am right! And *I* have to defend my rights.

Nor do we hear much about losing our lives. We fight hard to defend ourselves. We are advised to find ourselves—to seek self-fulfillment no matter what the cost to others. But Jesus' way is just the opposite. He says if we want to be His disciples, we have to deny ourselves (die to self) and take up our cross and follow Him. He also says if we try to save our life, we will lose it, but if we lose our life (die to self) for His sake, we will find it. This means obeying Him, putting others before ourselves in certain situations, giving up our rights for the benefit of others, and not having to be right all the time. This also means not putting other people down or walking over them in our search for fulfillment and our striving for achievement.

What is Jesus asking of us in our individual situations? It may be that we are in the wilderness because we haven't heeded Jesus' words in Matthew 16:24-25.

PRAYER: Help me, Lord, to accept these hard things that are my crosses in life. Help me to remember it is in dying to self that I will ion.

Related verses: Deuteronomy 8:2; Luke 14:27; Philippians 2:3-8, 3:7-11

SUFFICIENCY IN GOD

"Not that we are sufficient of ourselves to think anything as of ourselves, but our sufficiency (competence, NIV) is of God." 2Corinthians 3:5

Sometimes it takes a wilderness experience to show us how dependent we are on God. Lamentations 3:22 tells us if it weren't for His mercy, we wouldn't even be alive. Yet many people go on day after day in their own self-sufficiency, never realizing their need of God. "We're strong," they think, "and able to carry on by ourselves." When we have that attitude we miss what God can do for us. The Danish philosopher, Kiarkegaard, said, "To need God is [our] highest perfection. [Our] highest achievement is to let God be able to help."

In the wilderness we realize our sufficiency is of God. We have tried to manage in our own strength and wisdom, but failed. We depended on our own sufficiency and let ourselves down. We now see that when we depend on God and let Him be our sufficiency, He doesn't ever let us down.

God is never-failing (Deuteronomy 31:6). His compassions are new every morning and great is His faithfulness" (Lamentations 3:22-23).

PRAYER: Father God, keep us aware of our need for You and help us to let You be our sufficiency.

Related verses: Joshua 1:5; 1 Chronicles 28:20; Psalm 40:17, 55:22; John 10:27-29; Philippians 4:19; Hebrews 13:5

NO FEAR OF DEATH

".. *T*hat through death he [Jesus] might destroy him that had the power of death, that is, the devil; And deliver them who through fear of death were all their lifetime subject to bondage." Hebrews 2:14-15

One big wilderness-causing factor in our lives can be the fear of death. Those of us who have struggled—or are struggling—with this fear know the panic caused by an ache or pain of unknown origin. We know the debilitating effects of having to wait to find out the cause. We know the grip of fearing the worst and the bondage it causes.

But we need not continue to live in fear of death. Jesus died to deliver us from that fear. When we look to Him and trust Him in those times of uncertainty, He can remove the fear that has enslaved us for so long.

I know—because He did it for me. From my teenage years till mid-life, I was a true hypochondriac. Every little ache and pain caused me to fear the worst. My mother's dying of breast cancer when I was three probably contributed to my fear of death. Then in a more-than-imaginary time of fear when I was scheduled to have a biopsy on a breast lump, I sought God and by the scheduled date He brought me to a place of perfect peace. I could say along with Job and my mother, "Though he slay me, yet will I trust in him" (Job 13:15). I rejoiced that God had delivered me from the fear of death that had bound me for so long.

It has been said that until a person accepts death, they can't really live. Living in fear of death prevents us from experiencing the joy of living.

PRAYER: Jesus, I'm tired of being afraid of death. Help me as I seek You for deliverance, and please bring me to a place of peace.

Related verses: Psalm 23; Isaiah 25:8; Romans 8:38-39; 1 Corinthians 15:54-57

REST

"For he that is entered into his rest, also hath ceased from his own works..." Hebrews 4:10

The fourth chapter of Hebrews has a lot to say about our entering into God's rest. While the writer is talking about the rest we will have at the end of our lives when we go to Heaven, part of verse 10 could hold an additional message for us. It could be saying we enter into rest (of mind and spirit) when we cease from our own works and do what *God* wants us to do.

We humans have strong wills. We know what we want to do. We have our hearts set on doing a certain thing: getting a certain degree, taking a certain job, marrying that certain person, or fulfilling a certain ambition. We want what we want! And we work hard at getting what we want. Our minds and spirits stay in turmoil as we seek to reach our goals. Because of the stress, we may end up in the wilderness.

But what about what *God* wants us to be doing? Have we sought *His* will for our lives? Are we doing what we know *He* wants us to be doing?

Perhaps verse 10 is telling us when we give up our *own* wants and desires, and seek *God's* will, life is so much more peaceful. When we cease from doing our own work—striving to do what *we* want to do— we find a rest of spirit, mind, and body.

PRAYER: Help me, God, to take time from my busy self-seeking to look to You and find what *You* want me to be doing. Thank You for Your promise of rest.

Related verses: Proverbs 3:5-6; Matthew 7:21-23; Luke 22:42; John 5:30; 1 Corinthians 4:19, 16:7; Ephesians 5:17; James 4:13-15; Hebrews 13:20-21

HOW OFTEN FORGIVE

"... 'Lord, how many times shall I forgive [someone] when they [sin] against me? Up to seven times?' Jesus answered, 'not seven times, but seventy-seven times.'"Matthew 18:21-22

It happened again! A person close to me failed to do something that was important to me. This had become a pattern through the years. *How much longer can I take this?* I wondered.

It's usually the long-term, on-going situations (work situation, marriage, family) that require continuing forgiveness—over and over again. A one-time incident—depending on the "sin"—is easier to forgive. But Jesus talks about the more-than-once situation. Should we keep on forgiving the same person? For the same transgression? Jesus says we are to keep forgiving, even if it's too many times to count.

Unforgiveness can send us into the wilderness, and refusing to forgive causes resentment and bitterness toward the person at fault. Unforgiveness ruins relationships. We would do well to ask ourselves: *Which is more important—the issues, or my relationship with that person or persons?* Jesus knew relationships are more important. That's why He said to keep on forgiving.

So once again I choose to forgive. I also ask God to take away the resentment and bitterness I feel. And once again, He does.

PRAYER: O God, it's so hard to keep on forgiving the same person for the same thing. But with Your power I can do it. Thank You that you take away the bitterness and resentment too.

Related verses: Matthew 6:12-15; Luke 6:36-37; Ephesians 4:32; Colossians 3:12-14

GOD'S PLAN

"*O*Lord, I know it is not within the power of man to map his life and plan his course." Jeremiah 10:23 (The Living Bible)

Is it possible for us to plan our own destiny? According to Jeremiah, we don't have the power to map out and plan the course of our own lives.

God wants to lead us in *His* plan for our lives. Psalm 32:8 (The Living Bible) says, "I will instruct you (says the Lord) and guide you along the best pathway for your life; I will advise you and watch your progress."

But sometimes we go our own way and find ourselves in the wilderness. The Children of Israel ended up in the wilderness for the very same reason. They didn't want to follow God's plan for going into the Promised Land, but rather chose to do it their way. So God had to allow them to wander in the wilderness for 40 years.

God sometimes has to allow us to wander in the wilderness for awhile too. There are things we need to learn, just as the Children of Israel did. But God doesn't leave us alone in the wilderness. He promises He will always guide us (Psalm 48:14), as He guided the Children of Israel (Psalm 78:52), and will lead us in His plan for our lives.

The best way is to seek God and to follow His way. But if we get sidetracked into the wilderness, there is still hope. "And if you leave God's paths and go astray, you will hear a Voice behind you say, 'No, this is the way; walk here'" (Isaiah 30:21, The Living Bible). God wants us to cry to Him in the wilderness so He can deliver us out of our distress and lead us forth by the right way (Psalm 107:4-7).

PRAYER: Lord God, You know the best plan for my life. Please forgive me for going my own way, and lead me back into Your plan.

Related verses: Joshua 1:5; Psalm 139:9-10; Proverbs 3:5-6; Isaiah 48:17; John 10:3-4

DISCIPLINE

"For whom the Lord loveth he chasteneth [disciplines], and scourgeth every [one] whom he receiveth." Hebrews 12:6

In Hebrews 12 we're told if we are children of God, then God will discipline us. How does God do that? By making life all "sunshine and roses"? That would hardly be discipline.

No, God chastens or disciplines us by allowing hard things in our lives. He allowed the Children of Israel to wander in the wilderness and He allows wildernesses in our lives at times too. The Psalmist stated it thus: "I know, O Lord, that thy judgments are right, and that thou in faithfulness hast afflicted me" (Psalm 119:75). Earlier, the Psalmist said before he was afflicted he went astray, but afterwards he kept God's word (v.67). In verse 71 he says, "It is good for me that I have been afflicted; that I might learn thy statutes." The Psalmist recognized and knew God's discipline.

Do we recognize God's discipline in *our* lives? Do we see trials and hard times as being from a loving God who cares so much for us that He wants to help us grow into mature Christians? Hebrews 12:10 tells us God disciplines us for our good so we may share His holiness.

When we submit to our heavenly Father's discipline, we follow Jesus' example who "though he were a Son, yet learned he obedience by the things which he suffered" (Hebrews 5:8).

PRAYER: Father God, thank You that You know what I need in order to grow into maturity. Thank You, too, that I can be sure the discipline from Your loving hand is right for me.

Related verses: 2 Samuel 7:14; Psalm 118:18, 94:12-14; Hebrews 12:5-11

PARTAKERS OF CHRIST'S SUFFERINGS

"*B*ut rejoice, inasmuch as ye are partakers of Christ's sufferings..." 1 Peter 4:13

There are numbers of verses in the New Testament which speak of our being a part of Jesus' sufferings. Philippians 3:10 says: "That I may know him...and the fellowship of his sufferings." Romans 8:16-17 says we are the children of God—heirs of God—and joint-heirs with Christ, if we suffer with him. "The sufferings of Christ [abounding] in us" is mentioned in 2 Corinthians 1:5.

When the Apostle Paul wrote those verses, there was widespread persecution of Christians and it was easy to define "suffering with Christ." Today, most of us don't have that kind of persecution. So how are we part of Christ's sufferings?

When trials, hard times, and wilderness experiences come our way and we hang in there doing what we know God wants us to do, we are "partakers of Christ's sufferings." If we are in the place of work God has for us and there are relationships that continually cause us grief and challenge us to respond with the love and grace of Jesus, then we are being part of Jesus' sufferings. If we are in a marriage that is less than ideal, but we accept the lack we feel and choose to love unconditionally—in obedience to the Word—then we're being a part of the "fellowship of His sufferings." If we are rejected by friends or family (or someone else) for doing or saying what we know is right, we are partakers of Christ's sufferings.

These times of suffering may seem long and often unbearable, but 2 Timothy 2:12 (NRSV) says if we endure, we shall reign with Christ.

PRAYER: Help me to rejoice, Lord Jesus, that I have the privilege of suffering with You. And help me to endure.

Related verses: Acts 5:41; 1 Corinthians 4:11-13; 2 Corinthians 1:5-7, 4:8-11,17-18; 2 Thessalonians 1:4-5; James 5:10; 1 Peter 4:12-14, 5:10

CONTENTMENT

"... *I* have learned, in whatsoever state I am, therewith to be content." Philippians 4:11

Do we ever truly learn contentment? It would appear that the Apostle Paul did.

But how many of us have come to the place of true contentment?

For many of us, learning contentment is a life-long struggle. And just when we think we've learned it, we find ourselves in a situation that causes discontentment to rear its ugly head again.

We may go to visit someone with an elegant house. Our friend shows up in a beautiful new outfit. We find ourselves in a group of people who seem to "have it all together" or who are more "polished" or more educated than we are. Many things can cause us to feel discontentment, and especially so when we're already in the wilderness.

Usually discontentment comes from comparing ourselves with other people.

2 Corinthians 10:12 indicates that people who "measure themselves by themselves and compare themselves among themselves" aren't wise. When we compare ourselves and our situations with others, it can either cause us to be discontent—or more content, depending with whom we're comparing ourselves. As long as we're discontent, we can't accept ourselves and our situation.

Focusing on the positive aspects of our situation and developing an "attitude of gratitude" for who we are and what we have, helps us to be content. Considering people in third-world countries can also help to get our contentment back into perspective.

PRAYER: Lord God, Provider of all, help me to learn to be content with myself as you have made me and with my situation as You have allowed it to be.

Related verses: Proverbs 15:16; Matthew 6:19-21; Luke 12:15; 1 Thessalonians 5:18; 1 Timothy 6:6-10; Hebrews 13:5

FRUITFUL IN AFFLICATION

"... *G*od hath caused me to be fruitful in the land of my affliction." Genesis 41:52

If life ever threw anyone a cruel blow, it was to Joseph. Sold by his brothers when he was only a young boy, made to live in a strange land among strange people, framed by Potiphar's wife and put into prison. How much worse could it be? But Joseph remained true to God and God was with Joseph and used his trials and hardships to mature Joseph and to prepare him for God's service. Eventually, Joseph was able to say God caused Him to be fruitful in the land of his affliction.

God can do the same for us. What are our afflictions, trials, and hardships? Are we letting God cause us "to be fruitful in the land of [our] affliction?" Being fruitful depends on how we accept our problems and hardships. If we face them merely with a "resigned" acceptance, we fail to be fruitful in hard times. But if we face our "affliction" with creative acceptance, we can be fruitful no matter what comes.

One elderly woman who is too weak to leave her house, corresponds with prisoners. A young girl with many physical problems that sometimes cause her to despair, concentrates on speaking a word of encouragement to everyone she talks to. Another person who experiences many disappointments and times of discouragement, offers a listening ear and warm caring to other hurting people.

No matter how hard our situation, there are things we can do to minister to others if we will just look for them. At the very least (or should I say "most") we can pray for others. Prayer is a powerful force and much needed. What better way to be creative and fruitful in the land of our affliction?

PRAYER: Lord God, show me how to be fruitful in carrying out Your purposes in spite of my own trials and hardships.

Related verses: John 15:1-2; Colossians 1:9-14

OUR COMFORTER

"*B*lessed be God...the God of all comfort; Who comforteth us in all our tribulation, that we may be able to comfort them which are in any trouble, by the comfort wherewith we ourselves are comforted of God." 2 Corinthians 1:3-4

Where do we go for comfort when we're in the wilderness and we're hurting, suffering, sorrowing, or afflicted? God, our merciful Father and all-comforting God, wants to console and comfort us. God comforts us through the Holy Spirit (Acts 9:31), through His Word (Romans 15:4), and through His people (1 Corinthians 14:3; 2 Corinthians 7:13). God wants to comfort us so we'll know how to comfort and console other people who are in trouble. If we don't go to God and let Him comfort us in our hard times, we can't comfort or console others with God's comfort when they're in trouble.

None of our experiences of hurting, suffering, sorrow, or affliction are ever wasted if we let God use them for His honor and glory. And it is certainly to His honor and glory when we comfort others in trouble.

PRAYER: Lord God, thank You for Your comfort in my hard times. Enable me to pass on Your comfort to others when they're in trouble.

Related verses: Isaiah 49:13, 51:3 (substitute your name for Zion), 54:11, 66:13; John 14:26; 2 Thessalonians 2:16-17

RESULTS

"... Master, we have toiled all the night, and have taken nothing: nevertheless at thy word I will let down the net." Luke 5:5

Are you in the wilderness because you have tried to do your best in the thing you feel God wants you to do, but it seems you're not getting anywhere—or have failed? Perhaps you're thinking, *Nothing I do works out or produces results. I may as well quit*! Are you like the disciples, who worked all night to catch fish but didn't even catch *one* (Luke 5:5)? Then along came Jesus and told them to put their nets down again. The disciples were tired by then and didn't feel like trying again so soon. They probably didn't have much faith that anything would happen. But they chose to obey Jesus and they caught so many fish that the net broke.

Are you feeling like those disciples? Tired? You don't feel like keeping on with what you're doing? You're not sure you're even supposed to keep on—much less *how*?

God doesn't ask *results* of us. *He* is the one who gives the results (1 Corinthians 3:7). All He asks of us is that we continue to be obedient and faithful in the thing He has called us to do.

PRAYER: Lord Jesus, I don't see results in my work for You, and I'm weary. Nevertheless, I will continue to be obedient and faithful in this task You have called me to do.

Related verses: Isaiah 55:11; Galatians 6:9; 2 Thessalonians 3:13

FULNESS IN CHRIST

"*As* sorrowful, yet always rejoicing; as poor, yet making many rich; as having nothing, and yet possessing all things." 2 Corinthians 6:10

Can we *really* be sorrowful and yet rejoice? Poor, yet still make others rich? As having nothing, yet possess all things? I believe we can.

There have been times in my life when I've had disappointments, hurts, and rejections, and these caused deep sorrow. And yet I found I could still joy in the Lord, even at the time I was feeling sorrowful.

I've been poor financially at times, and yet there were things from our huge garden that I could share with many people. I have felt poor emotionally and spiritually, yet I found I could still enrich others by providing a listening ear and showing compassion for them in their hard times. I could share the wisdom and comfort God had provided for me in my hurting times.

I have experienced feeling that my possessions are unimportant, but because I have the fullness of Christ, I have everything. The things in life are *only things* and our treasure in heaven is what counts.

With this kind of living comes true freedom and release. The feelings of sorrow, being poor, and having nothing are not binding, but rather liberating when accompanied by joy, sharing, and knowing we have everything (fullness) in Christ.

PRAYER: Thank You, Jesus, for the freedom I have in You, that even hard things in life need not bind me and keep me from Your fullness.

Related verses: Ephesians 3:14-21, 4:13; Colossians 1:18-19, 2:9-10

REJOICE ALWAYS

"Rejoice in the Lord always. I will say it again: Rejoice!" Philippians 4:4 (NIV)

When life is going well, it's easy to rejoice. But Paul says to rejoice in the Lord *always*. Always? Even when life is hard? When our situation seems impossible? When our hearts are breaking? When with every breath we want to cry, "Enough! I can't take anymore"? Even in the wilderness?

According to God's Word, even in *those* times, we're to rejoice. Paul wrote, "sorrowful, yet always rejoicing" (2 Corinthians 6:10, NIV), "exceeding joyful in all our tribulation" (2 Corinthians 7:4, KJV), and "we glory in tribulations" (Romans 5:3).

How can we be joyful in sorrow, in tribulations? Galatians 5:22 gives a clue: "the fruit of the Spirit is joy." A further clue is found in Psalm 16:11, (NRSV): "In Your presence there is fullness of joy." The way to joy, even in hard times, is to spend time with God and let the Holy Spirit fill us. We can't produce joy on our own. It has to be a fruit of the Holy Spirit in us, and it only comes through being in God's presence. Then we have true joy that remains even when the going gets tough.

PRAYER: Thank You, Holy Spirit, for Your joy no matter what life brings my way. Help me to allow You to produce that joy in me.

Related verses: Psalm 31:7-8, 63:7; Colossians 1:24; 1 Thessalonians 5:16; 1 Peter 1:3-9, 4:12-13

NO BLAME

"... *L*et every [person] be swift to hear, slow to speak, slow to [anger]." James 1:19

Perhaps there is a situation in our lives that periodically drives us into the wilderness. We don't like the situation. We wish we didn't have to put up with it. We wish we could change it, but another person controls it. We could leave the situation, but we know God wants us to "stay put." In fact, God may have told us not to blame that person because that person is His (God's) instrument to teach us. That makes it hard! We still feel like "copping out" at times. We still want to blame.

Perhaps we've been in this situation a long time and it doesn't get any easier. We realize God has taught us many things and it appears there is still more He wants us to learn. Does He want us to quit blaming? Maybe we haven't been blaming right out, but we've still been blaming in our hearts. And at times we're tempted to shout accusations at "that person."

Jesus gives us an example of how to respond when we want to blame someone else for our hard situation. "When He was abused, he did not return abuse; when he suffered, he did not threaten; but he entrusted himself to [God] who judges justly" (1 Peter 2:21-23, NRSV). Can we do the same?

PRAYER: O God, this situation is so hard. Please enable me to accept and love and not to blame. Help me to be like Jesus. I commit myself and my situation to You, Lord God.

Related verses: Isaiah 53:7; Ephesians 4:31-32; Hebrews 12:3

WHOM BUT GOD?

"*W*hom have I in heaven but thee? and there is none upon earth that I desire beside thee." Psalm 73:25

What kind of relationship do we have with God? Is it a casual relationship that believes God exists and we recognize Him once in awhile? Is our relationship with God only the pray-to-Him-when-I-need-Him kind? Do we read God's Word once a day and then forget about Him the rest of the day? Or is our relationship with God so vibrant that we can say with the Psalmist, "Whom have I in heaven but thee? and there is none upon earth that I desire beside thee?"

Do we enjoy sharing our joys and high moments with God and also turn to Him right away when problems arise and the low times come? Do we spend much of our free time (when we're not having to concentrate on what we're doing) thinking of—and communing with—God?

God longs to have first place in our lives, even above our earthly relationships. In fact, He *requires* that we put Him first. Our highest desire should be for God. And when our desires are in line, our earthly relationships will be enhanced.

PRAYER: Lord God, my relationship with You needs to be in first place. Purify my desires so I desire You above all other relationships and things.

Related verses: Psalm 139:17-18; Matthew 6:33

THANKSGIVING

"*Enter* into his gates with thanksgiving, and into his courts with praise: be thankful unto him, and bless his name." Psalm 100:4

How do we come before God? Do we rush right in with all our intercessions and petitions? The Psalmist says we're to "enter his gates with thanksgiving and into his courts with praise." He further states we're to "be thankful unto him and bless his name."

When we're in the wilderness, we sometimes feel we don't have anything to be thankful for. But it does something to us—and for us—when we thank and praise God. Even when we don't feel able to see any blessings, just saying, "Thank You, God, Praise You, Lord" (or similar expressions) over and over can be therapeutic because it somehow sends the message to our minds and reminds us that we *are* blessed.

Thanking, praising, and worshipping God gives us entrance into the presence of God, and opens the way for our petitions and intercessions. God deserves our thanks and praise no matter what our circumstances or how we feel, because God never changes.

Lamentations 3:23 says His mercies are new every morning and great is His faithfulness! What better reason do we need for thanking and praising God?

PRAYER: O Lord, I come into your presence with thanksgiving and praise. Thank You for Your great faithfulness. Related verses: Psalm 50:14-15, 95:1-3, 107:21-22; Colossians 4:2

CALL ON GOD

"*He* shall call upon me, and I will answer him: I will be with him in trouble; I will deliver him, and honour him." Psalm 91:15

Prayer—that wonderful avenue to God! But sometimes in the wilderness we think, *Why pray? It won't do any good anyway!* When we're in the depths, we may even feel that God doesn't hear us.

The Psalmist experienced these feelings. He felt cut off from God. But he found when he cried unto God, God heard him (Psalm 31:22). The writer of Lamentations also felt "cut off." But he testifies that when he called on God, God drew near and told him not to fear (Lamentations 3:54-57).

There are many instances of answered prayer in the Bible. The prayer of Jabez was answered, as we see in 1 Chronicles 4:10. Solomon asked a specific request of God and God gave it (2 Chronicles 1:7-12). In 2 Chronicles 14:11-12, Asa had a great need and cried unto God. God delivered Asa. These are only a few of the answered prayers recorded in the Bible.

There may be times when we feel we don't need to pray because God knows our thoughts anyway. Or we tell our needs to God "on the run." We may be surprised to find that when we finally stop and take time to really come before God and tell Him our needs and how we're feeling (even though He already knows), it makes a difference.

PRAYER: Lord God, thank You for Your promise to be with me in the wilderness and to answer when I call on You. Thank You for the way You're going to help me through this hard time.

Related verses: Psalm 4:1, 18:1-6, 50:15, 55:16; 65:2, 86:1-7, 145:18-19

WORRY? NO!

"*D*o not worry about anything, but in everything by prayer and supplication with thanksgiving let your requests be made known to God." Philippians 4:6, (NRSV)

In the wilderness we can get to the place where everything seems wrong. Everything worries and everything wearies. Things in our everyday lives that were always manageable before now loom as mountains. The problems of our children, friends, and others seem insurmountable. And the problems of the wider world appear as impenetrable fortresses—which indeed some of them are! All of life seems out of control. We feel we just have to *do something* to change every situation. But in reality we find we can change *nothing*.

What do we do? We do what we should have been doing all along. We heed the teaching in Philippians 4:6 (NRSV): "Do not worry about anything, but in everything by prayer and supplication with thanksgiving let your requests be made known to God." What is the result of doing that? "And the peace of God, which surpasses all understanding, will guard your hearts and your minds in Christ Jesus" (v.7).

Perhaps if we had heeded this advice right from the beginning when we first started to worry, we wouldn't be in the wilderness now. But it's never too late to start and to persist, so we can get back to feeling normal again. And let's not forget to include "with thanksgiving." That is needed for our healing also.

PRAYER: O God, I'm so tired of worrying. Please enable me to tell You my requests with thanksgiving and to trust You for the peace You give.

Related verses: Isaiah 26:3; Luke 10:38-42 (NRSV); John 14:27, 16:33

GOD'S LOVE—GOD'S DISCIPLINE

"... *T*he Lord disciplines those whom he loves, and chastises every child whom he accepts." Hebrews 12:6 (NRSV)

"Does God *really* love me? If so, why does He allow these hard times?"

These are typical questions in the wilderness. Hebrews 12:6 says God *does* love us and that's why He disciplines us. Therefore, we are not to "regard lightly the discipline of the Lord or lose heart when [we] are punished by him." We're also told to "endure trials for the sake of discipline" (v.7).

We usually think of discipline as what is required when we do wrong. But there may be maturing or refining God knows we need. Do we have attitudes, motives, and desires that need changing? Maybe we've been trying to do things on our own instead of depending on God. God wants us to be dependent on Him (Proverbs 3:5-6). Maybe we need to learn to trust Him in a deeper way and to give our worries, fears, and problems to Him immediately as they come instead of letting them cause turmoil in our minds. Many times this turmoil is a major cause of our getting into the wilderness.

Whatever the reason for our wilderness, God's love is always sure (Romans 8:38-39). God loves us so much He disciplines us so we can share His holiness (Hebrews 12:10). When we subject ourselves to God's discipline and open ourselves to what He has to teach us, we will be rewarded with "the peaceable fruit of righteousness" (v.11).

PRAYER: O God, this discipline hurts! But I want to learn the lessons You know I need to learn. Thank you for your great love.

Related verses: Psalm 94:12; Proverbs 3:11-12; Revelation 3:19

DARK VALLEYS

"... Though I walk through the valley of the shadow of death, I will fear no evil: for thou art with me; thy rod and thy staff they comfort me." Psalm 23:4

In the wilderness there may be times when we feel like we're walking through "the valley of the shadow of death." We feel all is hopeless. Nothing will change, so why go on? We long for night when we can go to sleep—at least for a little while—and forget all our troubles. We dread getting up in the morning, knowing we will have to face the same hard situation. How can we bear it? Psalm 23:4 (NRSV) tells us the Lord is with us in our darkest valley. We don't have to fear evil. And He comforts us.

The Psalmist knew feelings of death. In one of his hard times he felt as though he were being drowned (Psalm 42:7). Yet he declared the Lord would still be loving in the daytime and the Lord's song would be with him in the night and he would pray to God (v.8). The Psalmist sometimes felt God had forgotten him (v.9). But when all seemed hopeless, he talked to his own soul and said, "don't be discouraged. Don't be upset. Expect God to act." Then the Psalmist made this declaration: "For I know that I shall again have plenty of reason to praise him for all that he will do. He is my help! He is my God!" (v.11, THE LIVING BIBLE). That had to be a bold statement of faith because the Psalmist wasn't feeling very hopeful.

In our darkest valley, will we make a bold statement of faith? Will we say—and continue saying: "This, too, shall pass?" Yes, this, too, shall pass! It really will! Let's declare with the Psalmist: "I shall yet praise Him, who is the health of my countenance, and my God" (v.11, KJV).

PRAYER: Thank You, Lord, that You are my Shepherd and You're with me in this dark valley. Help me to trust You and to remember this too shall pass!

Related verses: Psalm 71:14; Isaiah 43:1-2 (substitute *your* name); Romans 8:33-39

QUICK! CRY TO JESUS!

"When [Peter] saw the wind boisterous, he was afraid; and beginning to sink, he cried, saying, Lord, save me." Matthew 14:30

There is a lesson for us in this experience of Peter's. What do we do when the "winds of life" blow hard against us? When someone is unfair to us, rejects us, criticizes us, and we are hurt and begin to feel low? What do we do when suddenly we're hit with a strong temptation to worry, fear, despair, or feel hopelessness and we begin to be afraid we can't cope? What do we do when life gets too heavy or "too much" and we begin to be afraid we won't make it?

In these kinds of situations, do we cry out to Jesus when we "begin" to sink—or do we neglect to call on God and try every other means to "come up out of the waves," all the while going under further?

When Peter saw the strong wind and was afraid, he cried to Jesus as he was *beginning* to sink and Jesus caught him (v.31). Peter didn't wait till he was halfway or three-fourths of the way under before he cried to Jesus to save him.

When we feel ourselves "beginning to sink" we need to turn to Jesus *immediately*, instead of waiting until we're so far in the depths that we feel hopeless of getting out.

PRAYER: O God, when I feel I'm beginning to sink, remind me to seek Your help immediately. Thank You that You are always there for me, just as You were for Peter.

Related verses: Psalm 34:17, 46:1, 138:3

WHAT TODAY?

"*My* times are in your hand…" Psalm 31:15 (NRSV)

Life seems so full and busy. Many people express how it gets busier all the time. Feeling constantly overwhelmed by all one has to do can be a sure way into the wilderness.

All of us feel the push of life. With so much waiting to be done, the pressure of "what should I do today?" is always with us. Once when I was feeling extra pushed by all I had to do, God spoke to my heart, "I give you time for everything I want you to do." What does this mean? Are we doing some things God isn't asking of us—at least for now? Does this mean I need to learn to say "no" to certain requests? Does this mean God doesn't want me to be "all things to all people"? That some priorities for others aren't God's priorities for *me?*

We need to pray each morning, "Please lead me to do what *You* want me to do today." And throughout the day, it's good to ask God, "What do You want me to do *now?*" It's difficult to have peace about all the tasks we don't get done. But if God gives us time for everything He wants us to do and if we're trusting Him to do that and trusting Him to lead us, then we have to let go of the frustration and guilt we're tempted to feel because of all the things yet to be done.

PRAYER: Lord, all time is Yours. Enable me to trust You to show me what You want me to do—and when.

Related verses: Exodus 13:21; Psalm 31:14-15, 61:1-2, 138:8, 142:3; Colossians 3:17

A MERRY HEART

"A cheerful heart is a good medicine, but a downcast spirit dries up the bones." Proverbs 17:22, (NRSV)

One of the reasons we sometimes find ourselves in the wilderness is because we let life become too heavy. Without being conscious of it, we start to take ourselves too seriously and don't allow for mistakes. We feel that everything depends on us. We have to pray right or our prayers won't be answered. We have to act just right or people won't like us. We have to be all things to all people. We can't relax even for a short time, but feel driven to keep busy because there are so many things needing to be done. Before long, we feel no joy in anything—only heaviness—and we end up in the wilderness.

The Bible says a merry heart does good like a medicine (KJV). And so it is. A good laugh can do wonders for a downcast spirit. If we find life has gotten too heavy, we may have to put forth conscious effort to lighten up. We need to look for things that make us laugh. We need to allow for our own mistakes and learn to say, "Oops, I goofed!" instead of inwardly condemning ourselves. We need to loosen up in mind and body. Turning on good music and dancing around the room (even though we may feel silly) or going for a brisk walk is very therapeutic. And while we're at it, thanking and praising the Lord helps in the "loosening up."

PRAYER: Lord God, show me what I can do to help lighten my spirit. Please bring me to the place of laughter again.

Related verses: Proverbs 15:13,15

FOR GOD'S GLORY

"*T*his sickness is not unto death, but for the glory of God, that the Son of God might be glorified thereby." John 11:4

Jesus made the statement in John 11:4 when Mary and Martha sent word to Him that their brother, Lazarus, was ill. And then the Bible tells us although Jesus loved Martha and her sister and Lazarus, He stayed yet two days where He was (v.5-6).

Jesus had a purpose for making Mary and Martha wait. He chose not to respond immediately to the need so God could be glorified.

Might not it be the same with us? We become ill, or some other hard situation comes into our lives. Perhaps it is a real wilderness experience. We go to God and ask for healing or that our situation be changed. But it seems God doesn't answer. We wait. Can we believe God has a special purpose for not answering immediately? Might it be He wants to receive glory from our situation in a way different from what we think it should be? We know He loves us, as He did Mary, Martha, and Lazarus. Perhaps a more appropriate prayer would be, "Lord, show me how I can bring glory to You through this wilderness experience." Our goal should be to bring honor and glory to God in every situation that comes into our lives.

PRAYER: Father God, I want to honor and glorify You in this wilderness. Please show me how to do that.

Related verses: Psalm 96; Romans 4:20-21; 2 Corinthians 12:7-10

PRESERVED

"*H*e...preserveth the way of his saints." Proverbs 2:8

One of the tricks of our enemy, Satan, is to make people doubt their salvation. And he often uses this cunning strategy against older persons, even those persons who have loved and served God faithfully for many years. They read about or hear the glowing testimony of a person who had been deep in sin and who is now excited and joyful about their conversion experience. Then Satan whispers, "Maybe *you* never had a real conversion experience. Maybe you're just putting on a front." What a shock to the saint of God! If that saint doesn't recognize where these lies are coming from and doesn't "resist Satan" (James 4:7), Satan will continue to hound and beat him or her over the head with more and more lies until he has them in the wilderness.

Those who have accepted Jesus as their Savior, and are walking with God, need not believe the lies of Satan. God is able to keep what we have committed to Him until the day when we see Him face to face (2 Timothy 1:12).

PRAYER: Father God, thank You for saving me through Your Son, Jesus. Help me to believe Your Word that says You are preserving me (keeping my soul) forever.

Related verses: Psalm 103:10-12: Romans 8:1; Philippians 1:6; 1 Thessalonians 5:23-24; 2 Timothy 4:18; Jude 24-25

VICTORY

"*B*ut thanks be to God, who gives us the victory through our Lord Jesus Christ." 1 Corinthians 15:57 (NRSV)

There are bad happenings in the news every day. It's difficult to hear of people killing other people, and of floods, famine, and earthquakes. Even though we may not personally know the people affected, we feel sorry for them. When the bad news involves someone closer home— perhaps someone we know either casually or personally, it's harder yet. It's good we can feel for—and with—others in their hard times. But we need to be careful we don't let Satan use our feelings to get us down. This is especially true when we're in the wilderness.

Satan likes to take advantage of our vulnerability and tries to send our emotions and spirits to the depths. When he sees we're in a fragile state, he attempts to bring all kinds of things on us. He knows our weaknesses, the areas in which we struggle, and the things that tend to affect our emotions, and he will attempt to bring those into our already unsettled frame of mind. We need to be aware of Satan's tactics. When we're feeling fragile emotionally, we may have to consciously and with effort, distance our thoughts from "calamities" and make our refuge in the shadow of God's wings (Psalm 57:1). If we fix our hearts and trust in God, we don't have to be "afraid of evil tidings" (Psalm 112:7). In all of this, God will give us the victory through Jesus.

PRAYER: Lord God, I want to make my refuge in the shadow of Your wings. Thank You for giving me victory in Jesus.

Related verses: Colossians 2:15; Hebrews 2:14-15; 1 John 5:4-5; Revelation 12:10-11

SHAME

"...Jesus...endured the cross, despising the shame..." Hebrews 12:2

For some of us, part of carrying our cross is enduring the shame that goes with it. There may have been incidents in our family—or against ourselves—which cause shame. Tamar experienced this kind of shame and it affected her whole family (2 Samuel 13). Children may betray our beliefs and values and cause us to feel shame. There are legitimate reasons for people to feel shame and Jesus understands those feelings. He, the perfect Son of God, was treated—and put to death—as a criminal.

There are also feelings of shame caused by pride within ourselves. There are those women whose husbands aren't "polished" and may sometimes use incorrect English or talk in a way that embarrasses their wives. Or some husbands may not be organized and orderly and the surroundings show it. These things can cause women to feel shame. Feelings of shame that stem from pride can lead us into the wilderness.

We may be tempted to remove ourselves from those people or situations that cause us shame. But there is a better way. If we confess our pride, God will forgive us and cleanse us from it (1 John 1:9). It's humbling to admit it when our feelings of shame are caused by pride. But if we humble ourselves before God, He will lift us up (James 4:10) and will show us the way *He* wants us to feel about our situation.

PRAYER: O God, I confess to You my feelings of shame and pride. Please forgive me and help me to feel the way *You* want me to feel about my circumstances.

Related verses: Proverbs 11:2; Isaiah 50:6

SURRENDER

"...[*J*esus] threw himself on the ground and prayed, 'My Father, if it is possible, let this cup pass from me; yet not what I want but what you want.'" Matthew 26:39 (NRSV)

Surrendering to God means accepting our hard situation just as Jesus did His. Surrendering means no more "kicking against" our hard situation and it also means giving up our own efforts at trying to change it. Surrender is giving up our wants and desires for whatever God has for us in our situation. It means being willing for God to allow our situation to remain the same if that's what He knows is best for us. Surrender means putting our complete trust in God to work in the way—and the timing—He knows is best for us and everyone else in our situation.

Surrender means letting our attitudes, motives, actions, and reactions be directed by the Holy Spirit instead of by our feelings of anxiety, fear, hurt, self-pity, and discontent.

Surrender is not a one-time act. When something happens that triggers our negative feelings, we have to surrender *again*. Surrender is *continually* giving our situation to God and *leaving* it with Him. Surrender means believing that in all things God works together for our good (Romans 8:28).

PRAYER: O God, I want to surrender my will and my situation to You, but it's so hard when I'm in the wilderness. I need Your help.

Related verses: Matthew 6:10, 26:39,42; Mark 3:35; John 4:34; Romans 12:2; Ephesians 5:17

JUSTICE

"He is the Rock, his work is perfect: for all his ways are judgment: a God of truth and without iniquity, just and right is he." Deuteronomy 32:4

It's easy to become discouraged about our hard wilderness situation and about the situation of those around us—and in the world at large. The rich get richer and the poor get poorer. The weak become weaker and the strong dominate. Some people suffer one tragedy after another while others seem to go blissfully on with their lives. Sometimes we wonder: *Does God really love us if He allows such inequities? If God is a God of mercy and justice, why are things so unfair and out of balance?*

But even though we sometimes feel life isn't fair, and wonder if God really does love us, the Bible assures us God is a God of justice and also a God of steadfast love and faithfulness (Psalm 89:14, NRSV). God says He acts with steadfast love, justice, and righteousness in the earth because in those things He delights (Jeremiah 9:24, NRSV).

We can rest in the fact there is a day coming when all inequities will be judged. If we patiently continue to do good in spite of unfairness and hard situations, we will receive the reward of eternal life (Romans 2:6-11).

PRAYER: Father, I'm so glad I can depend on the fact that You are a God of justice. Help me to rest in knowing You have control of my life right now.

Related verses: 2 Samuel 22:31; Psalm 97:2, 145:17 (NRSV); Jeremiah 32:19; 1 Peter 1:17; Revelation 15:3

ALL FOR GOOD

"We know that all things work together for good for those who love God, who are called according to his purpose." Romans 8:28 (NRSV)

Many aspects of our hard situation may be because of another person. But there is something else to consider. It could be that God is using the other person to work out His plan in our lives. God has been known to do that from the beginning of time. God used Pharaoh's hardened heart to work out His plan for the children of Israel (Exodus 7:1-5).

Oswald Chambers wrote that there are no "second causes" with God. Edith Marshall, wife of Peter Marshall, Jr., said at one point she had been blaming Peter for a hard situation, and God spoke to her heart that her "beef" wasn't with Peter, but with God Himself, because He was allowing Peter to act as he was.

If we can see God as using our hard situation for our own good, it gives us a new perspective. It also eases the "down" feelings we have toward the other person and helps improve the relationship. We can waste so much of our lives blaming others for our problems and hardships, when all the time God is using those persons to accomplish His purposes in us. We are much farther ahead when we open ourselves to God's working in our lives and believe all things work together for our good.

PRAYER: Forgive me, God, for blaming _____ for causing my wilderness experience. I see now, that You are allowing my hard situation and I trust You to work all things together for my good.

Related verses: Genesis 50:15-20; Jeremiah 29:11

TRIAL OF OUR FAITH

"*I*n this rejoice, even if now for a little while you have had to suffer various trials, so that the genuineness of your faith…may be found to result in praise and glory and honor when Jesus Christ is revealed." 1 Peter 1:6-7 (NRSV)

The story of Joseph (Genesis 37-45) shows clearly how God uses the negative actions of others to carry out His purposes. Joseph tried to do good and met hardship at every turn. He checked on his brothers and they threw him into a pit and then sold him to some Midianite merchantmen going to Egypt. In Egypt he was put in jail for refusing a sexual advance, and was forgotten by a man who promised to seek his release.

If God loved Joseph, why did He allow one hardship after another in Joseph's life? If God loves *us*, why does He allow our hard situations to go on and on?

God used hard situations (caused by the negative actions of other people) to mature Joseph's faith, and Joseph trusted God and served Him in each situation. It is the same with us. God wants our faith to become genuine and strong and He allows wilderness situations in which our faith is tried. How else would our faith mature and become strong? God is more concerned about our faith and trust in Him than He is about our lives being comfortable and easy. We would do well to open our eyes of vision and believe God will use our hardships for His honor and glory, as He did Joseph's.

PRAYER: Lord God, please use this wilderness experience to make my faith genuine and strong.

Related verses: Matthew 8:23-26, 14:25-31; 2 Thessalonians 1:3-5; James 1:3

GOD'S MERCY

"*F*or he knows how we were made; he remembers that we are dust." Psalm 103:14 (NRSV)

God is a God of great mercy. Even though He spells out His expectations of us, He remembers we're human.

As the Children of Israel traveled through the wilderness, they disobeyed and provoked God many times, but Psalm 78:38-39 (NRSV) says, "Yet he, being compassionate, forgave their iniquity, and did not destroy them; often he restrained his anger, and did not stir up all his wrath. He remembered they were but flesh…"

As hard as we try to obey and follow God, we too, fail Him over and over. We worry when we should trust. We become anxious and fret instead of taking our requests to God with thanksgiving. We take matters into our own hands instead of waiting for God's way and timing. We continue to carry our burdens instead of casting all our care on Him. We don't acknowledge Him in all our ways and then wonder why things go wrong. We forget to thank and praise Him for His goodness and mercy.

God knows us. He created us (Genesis 2:7). Yet, God knows we as humans have the potential to make many mistakes. "Like as a Father pitieth his children, so the Lord pitieth them that fear him" (Psalm 103:13). Without God's mercy, none of us would make it.

PRAYER: Thank You, God, for remembering we're human, and thank You for having great mercy on us.

Related verses: Psalm 86:5, 13, 100:5, 103:8-12; James 5:10-11, NIV; Psalm 136

TOTAL COMMITMENT

"… *A*braham…Take your son, your only son Isaac, whom you love, and go to the land of Moriah, and offer him there as a burnt offering…'" Genesis 22:1-2 (NRSV)

Abraham was a man of God. But was his allegiance a shallow commitment, or was it total, no matter what? God had to test Abraham to see if he would be willing to give up everything important in order to follow God.

God sometimes tests *us* to see if we're willing to lay on the altar our most treasured dreams, desires, and relationships. The Apostle Paul counted all the important things in his life as "rubbish" in order to "gain Christ and be found in him" (Philippians 3:7-11, NRSV).

Is our happiness dependent on our dreams and desires being fulfilled, or on our relationship with God? Sometimes our dreams and desires stand in the way of knowing God. Our minds become so consumed with "wanting," that we forget what is most important. Jesus wants us to know Him personally, not just *about* Him. He wants our relationship with Him to be more important than having our dreams fulfilled or our desires met.

Abraham was willing to lay his most prized "possession," his desires, and his dreams on the altar because God was more important. What about *us*? Is our relationship with God important enough that we're willing to lay *all* on the altar?

PRAYER: O God, I want my commitment to You to be total, but it's so hard. Help me!

Related verses: Deuteronomy 13:3; Psalm 66:10-12, Matthew 16:24-27

GOD'S INSTRUMENT

"With all humility and gentleness, with patience, bearing with one another in love…" Ephesians 4:2 (NRSV)

We continue to struggle in our wilderness situation. It's not what we would choose at all. But circumstances and other people seem to control what happens in our lives. We can't seem to make our voice heard.

Could it be that God is allowing another person (whether housemate, co-worker, spouse, or whomever) to be His instrument to develop those characteristics in us that God knows we are lacking? For example, do we really love that other person or do we merely tolerate them? Do we continually show our displeasure for our situation by speaking or acting negatively toward them? Do we clam up and as much as possible ignore them and go our own way and do our own thing?

God wants us to truly love that person whom we feel is causing our wilderness situation. Love doesn't just tolerate another; it doesn't act negatively toward that person. Love doesn't clam up and ignore someone or go its own way and do its own thing.

How does our love for that other person measure up? God can use them as His instrument to teach us real (agape) love, if we let Him.

PRAYER: Lord God, help me to accept _____ as Your instrument. Enable me to love him/her with *Your* love.

Related verses: 1 Corinthians 13:4-8a; Colossians 3:12-14 (NRSV), 1 John 4:12

OUR THOUGHTS

"… The weapons of our warfare are…mighty through God… casting down imaginations…bringing into captivity every thought to the obedience of Christ." 2 Corinthians 10:4-5

Thoughts! Positive, negative, happy, sad, depressing, uplifting, kind, selfish, mean, and downright evil thoughts can come to all of us.

The struggle in our thought life is one of the hardest we face. We have no problem with the positive, happy, uplifting, and kind thoughts. We enjoy hugging them close and keeping them circulating in our mind. But it's those "other" thoughts that cause problems, especially when we're in the wilderness.

The negative, depressing, unkind, and even evil thoughts that bombard us are sometimes so shocking to ourselves that we would be ashamed to admit them to other people. We can't keep those kinds of thoughts from coming, but we are responsible for what we do with them.

Satan knows if he can get a foothold in our thoughts, he stands a chance of gaining control of our life. The longer we allow wrong thoughts to stay in our mind, the harder it is to become free of them. That's why it's so important to rebuke those thoughts *immediately* when they come and to seek God's help in replacing them with *His* kind of thoughts. Our weapons through God are mighty and can turn every one of our wrong thoughts into the kind God wants us to have.

PRAYER: O God, will You remind me to immediately rebuke wrong thoughts and to trust You to help me replace them with thoughts from You? Thank You, Lord.

Related verses: Psalm 51:10, 139:23-24; Proverbs 16:3, Philippians 4:8

LOVING OURSELVES

"[*J*esus said] …'You shall love your neighbor as yourself.' " Matthew 22:39 (NRSV)

We goofed. We really goofed! We missed a good opportunity, or said something "dumb," or did something we felt was stupid. And now we can't forgive ourselves.

For some of us, forgiving ourselves comes hard. But if I'm to love others as I love myself, what does it mean for me?

How do I love others? I'm not critical of them. I give them space to be human and to make mistakes. I forgive them. I even offer them a hug and an encouraging word.

Now, can I do that for *myself*? If I love myself properly, should I come down hard on myself when I make a mistake? Shouldn't I give myself space to be human? Shouldn't I forgive myself as I forgive others?

But forgiving myself is the hardest of all. I know God forgives me, but I find it so hard to forgive *myself*. Why do I think I have to be perfect? Is it because I'm thinking more highly of myself than I ought to think (Romans 12:3)? Do I think I should be above inadequacies and mistakes? Our worth to God doesn't change when we make mistakes, so why do we think less of ourselves? We need to trust that God has a purpose in allowing our "goofs" and that He will work everything for His honor and glory—even our mistakes.

PRAYER: O God, I have really goofed. I know *You* have forgiven me, but I can't seem to forgive myself. Please help me!

Related verses: Psalm 18:19, 103:13-14

SELF-LOVE and HUMILITY

"... *And* all of you must clothe yourselves with humility in your dealings with one another, for God opposes the proud, but gives grace to the humble." 1 Peter 5:5 (NRSV)

Yes, the Bible indicates we are to properly love ourselves so we can love others. But it also teaches dying to self (Matthew 16:24-25; 1 Corinthians 15:31), humbling oneself (Matthew 23:12), and not thinking more highly of ourselves than we ought to think (Romans 12:3).

It's hard to humble ourselves. There are situations in which we don't want to give in, give up—or just plain "give." We want our own way, do our own thing, have the last word. We have to be the winner. We don't like the feeling of being defeated, especially when we believe we're in the right. And when we're wrong, it's humbling to admit it.

But humbling ourselves and dying to self is where we find blessings. Proverbs 29:23(NRSV) says the person who is humble in spirit will obtain honor. According to Matthew 18:4, the person who humbles herself /himself as a little child is greatest in the kingdom of heaven.

Proper self-love and humility go hand-in-hand. When we have proper self-love, we are free to truly love others and to humbly interact with them.

PRAYER: Creator God, I need help to see the relationship between proper self-love and humility. Will You please show me?

Related verses: Psalm 10:17; Proverbs 16:19; Isaiah 57:15; James 4:10; 1 Peter 5:5-6

BELIEVING GOD'S LOVE

"*S*o we have known and believe the love that God has for us..." 1 John 4:16 (NRSV)

In order to have proper self-love with humility, we need to have a healthy self-esteem and self-worth. But when we're in the wilderness, we have feelings of inadequacy. We can't seem to keep up with all the demands of life. We find it hard to satisfy those close to us. Many things in our situation aren't as we'd like them, but we're helpless to change them. All in all, life is a drag most of the time. We're tired of it, but out hard situation continues. We find our self-esteem sinking and with it, goes our self-love.

Having a low self-esteem and little self-love makes it more difficult to bear our wilderness situation. To maintain a healthy self-esteem when the knocks of life come our way—and keep knocking—we have to seek God and stay close to Him. We have to know and believe our worth to God and His love for us. What are some of the ways we know God loves us?

God planned us before we were born (Psalm 139:13-16). God created us in His own image, after His likeness (Genesis 1:26-27). God chose us and ordained us (John 15:16). God loves us so much that He gave His only Son to die for us (John 3:16). Psalm 18:19 says God delights in us. We are graven on the palms of His hands (Isaiah 49:16). God calls us by name (John 10:3).

Knowing and believing God's love for us and our worth to Him, stabilizes our emotions and provides solid ground on which to stand in hard times.

PRAYER: O God, when I'm in the wilderness, it's so hard for me to believe you love me. Help me to believe.

Related verses: Psalm 42:8, 69:16; Jeremiah 31:3; 1 John 3:1, 4:19

HEALTHY SELF-ESTEEM

"... *D*o not think of yourself more highly than you ought, but rather think of yourself with sober judgment..." Romans 12:3 (NIV)

When we have proper self-love with humility, we know our self-worth in relation to our dependence on God. We know without Jesus we can do nothing

(John 15:5, NRSV). Our confidence rests in the fact that we can do all things (things He wants us to do) through Christ who strengthens us (Philippians 4:13). And we can say, "The Lord is my helper; and I will not fear what [anyone] shall do unto me" (Hebrews 13:6). Knowing our self-worth in God leads to a healthy self-esteem.

Having *low* self-esteem is not being humble. True humility is having a proper estimate of ourselves, which gives us a healthy sense of self-esteem as we recognize our strengths and weaknesses and accept ourselves as God made us. When we're able to accept ourselves as we are, we can more readily accept those situations in our lives that we can't change. A healthy self-esteem is also crucial to our having proper love for ourselves and to our having humility when relating to others.

PRAYER: Lord God, I want to see myself as *You* see me and to have a healthy self-esteem. Will You enable me to do that?

Related verses: Psalm 69:32-33, (TLB); 1 Corinthians 15:10

OUR HEART'S DESIRES

"*D*elight yourself in the Lord and he will give you the desires of your heart." Psalm 37:4 (NIV)

What does it mean to "delight" in the Lord? Delight means we take great pleasure in the Lord. We joy in Him and we find ecstasy and rapture in Him. Is this how it is with us? Do we find pleasure and joy in spending time with God or would we rather read a book, watch TV, or attend a sports event?

Perhaps there are times when we experience a certain pleasure and joy in God, but when He allows us to experience a hard situation or wilderness, even *that* delight in Him turns to frustration, uncertainty, and accusation. *God, why do You allow me to have these hard times? You don't seem to do anything about my situation. Do You love me or even care about me?*

What are the desires of our heart? If we've been in the wilderness a long time, perhaps our greatest desire is to be free of our circumstances. Do we desire release more than we desire a deeper relationship with God? Do we desire that another person change, instead of desiring that *we* grow and mature? Is our desire to have our own way stronger than our desire for God to have *His* way in our lives? Might it be possible that the desires of our heart would be different if we were delighting in the Lord? Perhaps God can't give us our heart's desires because those desires are tainted by our failure to delight in Him.

PRAYER: Lord, teach me to truly delight in You so my desires become the ones You will give me.

Related verses: Psalm 43:4; Habakkuk 3:17-18; Romans 5:11; 1 John 5:14

FEELINGS + THOUGHTS = ATTITUDES

"*S*earch me, O God, and know my heart: try me, and know my thoughts." Psalm 139:23

In the wilderness, our negative feelings run rampant unless we put forth strong effort to stop them. What can we do to abate these harbingers of despair?

First, we need to recognize we are totally dependent upon God. He is the One who can strengthen us inwardly (Colossians 1:11). In Psalm 27:14 we're told to wait on the Lord, be of good courage, and He will strengthen our hearts. While we're waiting, there is a formula we can follow: feelings + thoughts = attitudes.

When we have negative *feelings*, the kinds of *thoughts* we add to those feelings will determine our attitudes. If we have negative feelings and add negative thoughts to them, we end up with negative attitudes. But if we add *positive* thoughts to negative feelings, we open the way for God to give us positive *attitudes* (strengthen our hearts). We can't control what kinds of *feelings* come to us, but we can determine to think positive thoughts.

Positive thoughts include: *This is a hard situation, but with God's help, I will make the most of it. I know God is strong in my weakness* (2 Corinthians 12:9). *I can do all things through [Christ] who strengthens me* (Philippians 4:13, NRSV). Feelings + thoughts = attitudes, and our attitudes determine our response to life.

PRAYER: Lord God, I need You to strengthen my heart right now. Please show me how to apply positive thoughts to my negative feelings so I can have right attitudes.

Related verses: Proverbs 16:3; Philippians 4:8; Hebrews 4:12

OBEY

W"... e will obey the voice of the Lord our God…that it may be well with us…" Jeremiah 42:6

What do we do when a hard situation comes into our lives, such as a difficult marriage, or other trying relationship? As with all things, we have to work through our feelings and responses in the situation. More important than the working through, is *how* we work through it. Do we depend on our own inner resources or do we turn to God? If we depend on ourselves to resolve our feelings and determine our responses, we may insist that the other person change. We may feel like leaving the situation for awhile—or leaving for good. Or we may decide to cope as best we can by distancing ourselves in the relationship.

But if we turn to God for help and direction and are determined to obey Him no matter what, our responses are likely to be entirely different. Instead of seeking our own way and what *we* want, God tells us to seek the good of the other person (1 Corinthians 10:24, NIV). Instead of counting all the failures and wrongs of that person, we are to be kind and tenderhearted to him or her and to forgive that person as God forgives us (Ephesians 4:32). God tells us to forgive not just once but many, many times (Matthew 18:21-22). God tells us to love that person unconditionally (1 Corinthians 13:4-7).

If we turn to God and His Word, we will find the resources we need to obey God in our hard situation.

PRAYER: God, my situation is so hard, but I believe You want me to learn from it. Help me to be sensitive to Your leading and to obey.

Related verses: Psalm 32:10-11 (TLB); Matthew 5:46; Acts 5:32; Hebrews 5:9

CONTINUE IN PRAYER

"*C*ontinue in prayer, and watch in the same with thanksgiving." Colossians 4:2

Sometimes when we're in a hard situation, we tell God our troubles "on the run." We may think, *God knows my needs and what is bothering me, so why should I have to tell Him about them?*

It isn't until we stop and consciously come before Him and tell Him all about our problems and how we're feeling that we sense a difference in our inner being. Philippians 4:6-7 says we have to come to God in prayer, telling Him our requests along with thanking Him, and then He will keep our hearts and minds with His peace.

The Word speaks of prayer as a diligent act (Ephesians 6:18). Jesus felt the need of specific prayer and even continued all night in prayer at times (Luke 6:12). If Jesus needed that much communion with God, dare we think it's not important for *us* to spend periods of time with God? Might it be that we go into the wilderness when hard times come because we don't "continue in prayer, and watch in the same with thanksgiving?" Psalm 105:4, (NIV) tells us to "Look to the Lord and his strength; seek his face always."

PRAYER: Lord God, I do need to spend regular times in prayer with You. I can't go on without Your strength and help.

Related verses: Psalm 42:8; Luke 22:39-46; Acts 1:12-14; 1 Peter 4:7

PRAISE IN HARD TIMES

"As sorrowful, yet always rejoicing…" 2 Corinthians 6:10 (NRSV)

We've experienced hard situations and the wilderness. But have we known the despair and victory of Habakkuk 3:17-18 (NRSV)?

Habakkuk says that even though the fig tree does not blossom, and no fruit is on the vines; though the produce of the olive fails and the fields yield no food; though the flock is cut off from the fold and there is no herd in the stalls, "yet I will rejoice in the Lord; I will exult in the God of my salvation."

How could Habakkuk express this kind of faith in such a hard situation? What was the secret of his victory? Habakkuk tells us in verse 19: "God, the Lord is my strength; he makes my feet like the feet of a deer, and makes me tread upon the heights."

Habakkuk also indicates that praising and exulting God is a factor in not going under when difficult times come.

But it's hard to praise and thank God when we're in the wilderness. If so, we can offer the *sacrifice* of praise (Hebrews 13:15).

Praising and thanking God are important in the process of getting out of the wilderness. One way of doing this is to play praise and worship music and sing along with it. We can't do it just once and expect it to help. As Hebrews instructs, we have to *continually* offer the sacrifice of praise and in time, we will find ourselves with trust in God like Habakkuk had.

PRAYER: Lord God, teach me to put my faith and trust in You and to praise You in this wilderness.

Related verses: Psalm 71:12-14, 100:4-5; Romans 5:3-5, 14:17; Ephesians 5:18-20

GOD—WORTHY TO BE PRAISED

"From the rising of the sun unto the going down of the same the Lord's name is to be praised." Psalm 113:3

Do we want God just for what He does for us—or do we serve Him because He is *God*, the great God above all gods? If we want Him just for what He does for us, then we won't be able to praise Him when we're going through hard times because we'll feel He has let us down. But if we serve God and love Him because of who He *is*, then there will still be plenty to praise Him for—even in the wilderness. Our situation and the way we feel don't change the fact that God is the Creator of the world and all the beauty in it. God is still the sustainer of life (Job 2:10). If it weren't for God, we wouldn't be able to take another breath. God is the giver of every good and perfect gift (James 1:17), and He continues to love us (Jeremiah 31:3) even when we don't feel He is working in our behalf. In those times when we lack faith, He remains faithful to us (2 Timothy 2:13).

When we're in the depths, there is still much we can praise God for, and praise is an important part of our healing. It's our act of faith and it tells God we love Him and want to serve Him for who He is. It tells God we see Him as being worthy of our praise *always*, in every circumstance. God can use our praise to help in the process of bringing us out of the wilderness.

PRAYER: Help me, God, to love and serve You because of who You are and not just for what You do for me. I praise You because You are always worthy to be praised.

Related verses: Psalm 34:1-3, 96:1-9, 113:1-6, 145:9; Acts 17:22-28; Romans 11:36; Revelation 5:12

MATERIALISM

"… You cannot serve God and wealth." Matthew 6:24 (NRSV)

Am I materialistic? Does materialism cause wildernesses in my life?

We don't usually think of ourselves as being materialistic, but if we take a close look at our thoughts and actions, we may find we are more entrapped by materialism than we had thought.

Do we worry that some day we won't have enough money to live on? Do we spend more time in storing up earthly wealth than we do in that which will last for eternity? Do we have to keep up with other people in the kind of house we own, model of car we drive, and clothes we wear? Do we think of what we own as "ours" and forget that all in the heaven and in the earth is God's (1 Chronicles 29:11)? Do we congratulate ourselves for what we accomplish instead of recognizing honor comes of God and in His hand "it is to make great, and to give strength to all" (v.12)? When we give our tithes and gifts to God, do we remember all things are from God's hand and we are only giving back to Him what is already His (v.14)? Romans 11:36 says, "For of him, and through him, and to him, are all things: to whom be the glory forever." When we don't give God that glory, we are being materialistic.

Depending on material things instead of trusting God carries with it the possibility of failure. Worrying about the future prevents our enjoyment of today and erodes our trust in God's provision. Focusing on amassing material wealth gives only temporary satisfaction and sets us up for a letdown. Having to keep up with others can cause frustration and stress that ruins our peace and joy. If we remember we are but sojourners and our days are as a shadow (1 Chronicles 29:15), we will live as people preparing for our heavenly country. When we remember the earth and all in it is the Lord's (Psalm 24:1) and make sure material things don't take precedence over the spiritual in our lives, we are less likely to find ourselves in a materialism-caused wilderness.

PRAYER: O God, help me to remember everything good comes from You, and to give You the glory for it. Please show me how to keep the material in its proper place in my life.

Related verses: Matthew 6:19-21; Philippians 4:19; 1 Timothy 6:17-19

GOD'S WILL BE DONE

"... *T*hy will be done." Matthew 26:42

Many of us are creatures of habit. We like for things to always happen a certain way so life is predictable. When life is predictable, we feel in control. But let something—especially something hard—unexpectedly come into our lives and our feelings can change quickly. We are no longer sure of ourselves. We feel out of control. We become anxious and start to worry. We feel we have to change the circumstances and people in our situation. If we keep on this track, we eventually end up in the wilderness.

Jesus set the example for us when life seems out of control. Even though He became very heavy about His hard situation (Matthew 26:36-38), He did the best thing. He told God His desires (v.39), and then surrendered His will to God. A bit later He again told His Father, "thy will be done" (v.42). When life seems out of control, we would do well to fellow Jesus' example.

Instead of worrying and thinking we have to work things out ourselves, we're told to take our requests to God, *with thanksgiving*, and God's peace will keep our hearts and minds (Philippians 4:6-7). We don't always know what is best for ourselves and for those we're concerned about. As Romans 8:26 (NRSV) says, "we do not know how to pray as we ought," but we can surrender our will to God knowing the Holy Spirit is interceding for us and His interceding is according to God's will (vv.26-27). In confidence we can pray, "thy will be done."

PRAYER: Lord God, here are my desires. May *Your* will be done.

Related verses: Psalm 106:15; Jeremiah 10:23; Philippians 2:13

LOSS IS GAIN

I "... regard everything as loss because of the surpassing value of knowing Christ Jesus my Lord." Philippians 3:8 (NRSV)

Losses are disappointing—and sometimes frightening. The loss of a dream, our health, a job, a child, a friendship, or a marriage—are all difficult. But good can come from losses. Perhaps the person who has to give up a long-held dream finds great fulfillment in something different. Or for the person losing a job, there may be a better one ahead. The loss of health, a person close to us, a friendship, or a marriage can cause great anguish. In all losses, there's one common possibility—learning to know Jesus better, of drawing closer to God and experiencing a closer and deeper relationship with Him.

Prior to his encounter with Jesus, the Apostle Paul had many privileges and positions he could depend on (Philippians 3:4-5). But when Jesus spoke to him, he was willing to give up all those things he had put confidence in. And although he didn't actually have to give these privileges and positions up, he said, "what things were gain to me, those I counted loss for Christ (v.7). He further states, "More than that, I regard everything as loss because of the surpassing value of knowing Christ Jesus my Lord (v.8, NRSV).

Jesus wants us to learn to know Him better in *our* losses. Jesus wants to use our losses as stepping stones in drawing us to a more trusting relationship with Himself.

PRAYER: Jesus, help me in this time of loss to trust You completely. I want to have a deeper relationship with You.

Related verses: Mark 8:34-36; Philippians 3:7-11

PRACTICE GOD'S PRESENCE

"*And* take heed to yourselves, lest at any time your hearts be [weighed down] with…cares of this life… Luke 21:34

Life is so busy! It seems every season has its own particular things to keep us occupied and involved. And it never seems to get any better! The question is: *How do we keep everything in perspective, especially when we're in the wilderness?*

Jesus knew about the cares of this life and warned us not to let them become more important than preparing for His coming back to earth again (Luke 21:34). Jesus wants to be the center of our lives, and spending time with Him and in God's Word is the only way we can continue to keep Him as our main focus. When we're too busy to have a time of fellowship with God every day, we're indeed too busy.

Besides spending a daily time with God, we can "practice the presence of God" as we go about our activities and tasks. Making God a part of every aspect of our lives is a good way to stay out of the wilderness. When we share with Him our burdens, cares, sorrows, and disappointments right when they happen, He ministers to our spirits. And of course, He wants us to share with Him our joys, successes, and happy times too. Praising and thanking God continually helps to keep the sunshine in our souls by enabling us to keep the hard times in perspective. If we are already in the wilderness, practicing the presence of God is necessary to bring us out of our slump.

PRAYER: Lord God, thank You for Your constant presence with me. May I not get so busy with the cares of this life that I forget to take time to practice Your presence.

Related verses: Psalm 95:2; Proverbs 3:5-6; Mark 4:19; Luke 8:14

CHOOSE TO PRAISE

"*And* at midnight Paul and Silas prayed, and sang praises unto God: and the prisoners heard them." Acts 16:25

There sat Paul and Silas in prison with their feet in the stocks. They had just been attacked by a crowd, stripped of their clothes, and beaten unmercifully (Acts 16:22). Now they had to sit in one position with hurting bodies. What pain and agony!

How did Paul and Silas respond to this hard experience? They chose to pray and sing praises to God. Did they *feel* like singing and praying? Likely not. They may have felt forsaken by God. They may have felt their situation was hopeless. But they didn't live by their doubts and feelings. They chose to praise God in the midst of suffering. They chose to let the Spirit operate in them, which enabled them to sing psalms and hymns and spiritual songs among themselves, to sing and make melody in their hearts to the Lord and to give thanks always *for* all things (Ephesians 5:18b-20).

In our hard experiences we have the same choice Paul and Silas had. We can live by our doubts and feelings—or we can choose to praise God in the midst of our troubles. After Paul and Silas spent time praying and praising, God delivered them by opening the doors of the prison (Acts 16:26-40). When we spend time praising and thanking God in our hard times, it enables God to open the doors of our "prison" also.

PRAYER: O God, I choose to thank and praise You right now in the wilderness. I long for You to open the doors of my emotional "prison."

Related verses: Psalm 34:1-3; 103; Philippians 4:4

ROADMAP TO HEAVEN

"*Y*ou show me the path of life. In your presence there is fullness of joy; in your right hand are pleasures forevermore." Psalm 16:11 (NRSV)

We wouldn't think of taking a trip without first consulting a map for the right—and best—way to go. As we journey to heaven, we also need a "map" to tell us the right and best way to go. That map is the Bible—God's Word to us.

The Psalmist said God shows him the path of life. Do *we* depend on God's Word to show us the way in this life as we travel to heaven? Psalm 119:105 says: "[God's] word is a lamp unto my feet, and a light unto my path." If we don't depend on—and follow—our road map (the Bible) we will lose our way, just as we would lose our way if we didn't depend on and follow a map when we take a trip. The Psalmist was aware of that fact when he prayed, "Hold up my goings in thy paths, that my footsteps slip not" (Psalm 17:5).

Depending on and following God's Word is the best way to prevent our getting sidetracked into the wilderness. But if we do become sidetracked, the best way to get out is to consult our "map" and trust God to show us the way. Isaiah 30:21 (NRSV) says, "And when you turn to the right or when you turn to the left, your ears shall hear a word behind you, saying, 'This is the way; walk in it.'"

PRAYER: O Lord, I want to follow Your path out of this wilderness and on to heaven. Please show me the way as I depend on Your Word.

Related verses: Psalm 17:4, 18:30, 23:3,119:9,11,41; John 8:12

GIVE UP REGRETS

"But thanks be to God, [who gives] us the victory through our Lord Jesus Christ." 1 Corinthians 15:57

There they are again—those regrets about our having done something we shouldn't have done, or about something we should have done. We have asked God's forgiveness and we know He forgave us (1 John 1:9). But the shame and condemnation are again trying to play havoc with our minds. Where is this coming from? Certainly not from God, since He is our Justifier and sent Jesus to die for us. Jesus is even now at the right hand of God interceding for us (Romans 8:33-34). This shame and condemnation can only be from the accuser, the devil (Revelation 12:10). Should we then accept the shame and condemnation of those things that were nailed to the cross with Jesus? No! If we do so, we will be making Jesus' death to have been in vain. We will be taking back those sins and failures God has removed "as far as the east is from the west" (Psalm 103:12).

So let's choose to let go of the regrets. Let's choose to believe God can redeem our failures and mistakes and bring glory to His name in spite of them. Let's thank God He gives us victory through Jesus when Satan brings back the old regrets and tries to put condemnation and shame on us.

PRAYER: Lord, I cling to You and what You have done for me. Thank You for victory through Jesus.

Related verses: Luke 22:31-32; Ephesians 6:11; Colossians 2:15; 1 John 5:11

SATAN'S DEVICES

"*L*est Satan should get an advantage of us: for we are not ignorant of his devices." 2 Corinthians 2:11

What are Satan's devices? They are many. Are we aware that one of his most subtle devices is to cause division between persons? He wants to ruin the relationship between husband and wife, between friends, church members, and co-workers. Most of all, he wants to destroy the harmony between us and God.

One way Satan causes division is to plant resentment and bitterness in our hearts. In Hebrews 12:15, Paul warns about a "root of bitterness" springing up and causing trouble and tells us to pursue peace with everyone (v.14).

How do we keep bitterness from taking root within us when others cause us pain? 2 Corinthians 2:5-11 advises us to forgive and comfort the person who causes us pain and to confirm our love to them. We are to do this so we will not be outwitted by Satan (v.11, NRSV).

Satan comes to us with lies telling us we have the right to harbor resentment and bitterness—lies that we have to repay others for the hurt they've caused us. But God tells us to put away all bitterness, wrath, anger, [noisy complaints], evil speaking, and malice. Furthermore, we are to be kind one to another, tenderhearted, and to forgive one another (Ephesians 4:31-32). When we're tempted to have bitterness toward someone, do we obey Satan's lies or God's Word? Believing Satan's lies and letting bitterness take root in us will cause bondage, destroy our relationship with God, and lead us into the wilderness.

When we obey God's Word, we will know the truth and the truth will set us free (John 8:31-32).

PRAYER: O God, please take away these feelings of resentment and bitterness toward_____. Enable me to love him/her. Help me to want to obey Your truth.

Related verses: Psalm 25:4-5,10, 43:3, Matthew 5:43-46; Ephesians 6:10-18

DYING TO SELF

"... *Unless* a grain of wheat falls into the earth and dies, it remains just a single grain; but if it dies, it bears much fruit." John 12:24 (NRSV)

Dying to self is a necessary part of our Christian growth, just as a "grain of wheat" has to die in order to bring forth fruit. This death to self often occurs in the wilderness. Where normally we would be strong and able to carry out most anything we set our minds to, in the wilderness we feel weak, unstable, and finally come to the place where we know we are dependent on God. And that's where God wants us.

God wants us to be quiet and recognize Him in our lives (Psalm 46:10). He wants us to trust in Him with all our heart and not to go by our own understanding. He wants us to acknowledge Him in *all* our ways (Proverbs 3:5-6). God wants us to be willing to be taught and led by Him (Isaiah 48:17). Jesus wants us to know that without Him, we can do nothing (John 15:5).

Dying to self is hard. It hurts! But it's necessary if we want to be followers of Jesus. In Mark 8:34 (NRSV) Jesus says, "If any want to become my followers, let them deny themselves and take up their cross and follow me."

One way the wilderness facilitates dying to self is by ridding us of pride. Being in the wilderness is a humbling experience, but it's there God can do some of His best work in us if we let Him. God uses the wilderness to make us into the persons He wants us to become.

PRAYER: Lord, this dying to self is so hard, but please do Your work in me.

Related verses: 1 Corinthians 15:31 (NRSV); 2 Corinthians 3:18; Galatians 2:20

WHAT LESSONS?

"*I*t is good for me that I have been afflicted; that I might learn thy statutes." Psalm 119:71

Sometimes we find ourselves in the wilderness because of something we have done or because of wrong thinking. Such was the case with King Nebuchadnezzar. In spite of seeing God work in marvelous ways through Daniel, the King still didn't honor God in his own life. He took credit for Babylon being a magnificent city, built by his own mighty power and for his own majesty (Daniel 4:30). So God had to allow him to go through a terrible wilderness experience (literally) in order to teach him that God is sovereign over everyone and gives sovereignty to whomever He wills (v.32,NRSV). King Nebuchadnezzar had to learn it was God who had given him riches and greatness.

What are the truths and lessons God is trying to teach *us* in the wilderness? Do we need to learn to trust God in a deeper way? Is God more important to us than our health, wealth, and other people? Are we taking credit for the good things in our lives instead of giving God the credit for them? If we learn the lessons God is trying to teach us, then we will come forth saying, as King Nebuchadnezzar did, "Now I…praise and extol and honor the king of Heaven…" (v.37).

PRAYER: Lord God, please help me to learn the truths and lessons You want me to learn in this wilderness experience. May I soon be able to praise and extol and honor You with my whole heart.

Related verses: Daniel 4:28-37; Matthew 11:28-30; Hebrews 5:8

IN GOD'S WILL

"*N*ow may the God of peace…make you complete in everything good so that you may do his will…" Hebrews 13:20-21 (NRSV)

Sometimes when we're in the wilderness and can't seem to sense the presence of Jesus, it could be we're out of the will of God in some way.

Has God asked us to do something and we're not willing to obey Him? Is He requiring something hard of us and we're kicking against it? Perhaps He's asking us to love someone unconditionally, to give up our bitterness and resentment and forgive that person for hurting and disappointing us. Is He asking us to trust a rebellious teenager to Him instead of trying to have control ourselves? How about the sinful relationship we're involved in?

God desires to reveal Himself to us and to show us His will. But there are requirements for His doing so. John 14:21-23 indicates we have to keep Jesus' commandments and obey Him in order for Him to make Himself known to us and in order for Jesus and God to abide with us. Knowing God's will and submitting to it aids our getting out of the wilderness.

PRAYER: Lord God, I want to do Your will in this hard thing You're asking of me. Help me to give up my own will and follow You.

Related verses: Jeremiah 7:23; Matthew 7:21, 26:39; John 4:34; Romans 12:1-2; Philippians 2:13; Hebrews 13:20-21

IDOLS

"... *F*rom all your idols will I cleanse you." Ezekiel 36:25

There may be times when we're in the wilderness because of the idols in our lives. Not graven images (idols of gold and silver) such as the Old Testament mentions, but those things or people that are more important to us than is God. It has been said our "god" is anything or anyone that takes up more of our "think time" than God. And God states firmly in Exodus 20:3 that we're not to have any other gods before (besides) Him. God is a jealous God (v.5). He wants to be central in our lives and sometimes, in order for that to happen in us, we have to go through the wilderness.

But God is with us in the wilderness and He promises to give us a new heart and a new spirit (Ezekiel 36:26) and to put His Spirit within us and cause us to obey Him (v.27).

In the wilderness we see the futility of having idols, and we see it's only our relationship with *God* that really matters. We learn to put Him in His rightful place (above all else and anyone else). Then we are filled with the fullness of God and His power in us is able to do far above all we can ask or think (Ephesians 3:19-20).

PRAYER: All powerful God, I want You to be central in my life. Help me to put You above all else and everyone else.

Related verses: Psalm 51:2-3; Ezekiel 14:1-6; 1 John 5:21

KNOWING GOD AS OUR LOVING FATHER

"[*J*esus said], 'Pray then in this way: Our Father in heaven, hallowed be your name.'" Matthew 6:9, NRSV

God is our loving heavenly Father. But some of us have trouble thinking of Him as our *Father*. Perhaps our earthly father let us down at some important times in our life. He may have been insensitive to our needs. Perhaps he wasn't always there for us and caused us deep feelings of rejection. Or maybe we never knew our earthly father at all. In order to be able to think of God as our Father, we have to *know* God, not just *about* Him. And the only way we can know Him is by really knowing Jesus—not just *about* Jesus. Jesus said, "I and my Father are one…the Father is in me, and I in him…if ye had known me, ye should have known my Father also" (John 10:30,38, 8:19). To know Jesus is to know God.

Every person has the privilege of knowing at least *one* loving Father. When we see from the Bible who God really is and *what* He is—and then come to know Him personally, we can then believe it when we read He is our loving heavenly Father (John 16:27) and when it says Our Father in heaven is perfect (Matthew 5:48). We can believe He will never leave or forsake us (Hebrews 13:5), He is always sensitive to our needs and supplies those needs (Philippians 4:19), and He will love us always (Jeremiah 31:3).

PRAYER: God, the hurts from my earthly father are deep. Will You please heal my hurts and reveal Yourself as my loving heavenly Father? Thank You!

Related verses: Psalm 25:6, 68:5, 89:26; Isaiah 63:16; Matthew 7:11, 10: 29-31; 1 John 3:1, 4:16

SELF vs GOD

"... *I* die daily." 1 Corinthians 15:31

Life is hard. It isn't always fair. Some of us may be in a situation in which we don't want to remain. We're tempted to escape to something "better." The pull is strong. And yet, deep down, we know the Jesus way is to stay. To be willing to die to self (Matthew 16:24). To go the second mile (Matthew 5:41) and to be kind, tenderhearted, and forgiving just as God has forgiven us (Ephesians 4:32).

The self in us struggles to have its way and tells us, "I don't have to put up with this." God tells us to "endure hardness as a good soldier of Jesus Christ" (2 Timothy 2:3). Self says: "This hard situation will never improve." Jesus says: "with God all things are possible" (Matthew 19:26). Self says: I've gone too far to turn back." God says, "If we confess our sins, he is faithful and just to forgive us our sins, and to cleanse us from all unrighteousness" (1 John 1:9). Self says: "There's no purpose for me staying in this hard situation." God says, "suffering produces endurance, and endurance produces character, and character produces hope, and hope does not disappoint us" (Romans 5:3-5, NRSV).

God wants to use this hard situation to draw us closer to Himself, to bring us to a deeper trust in Him, and to mature us and prepare us for greater service. Will we let Him have His way with us—or will we leave for what we think would be "greener pastures"?

PRAYER: Help me, God, to put aside the self-arguments and to act on Your Word.

Related verses: Psalm 119:105; Proverbs 3:5-6; Matthew 16:24-25

DELIVERANCE

"*I* love the Lord, because he heard my voice; he heard my cry for mercy. Because he turned his ear to me, I will call on him as long as I live." Psalm 116:1-2 (NIV)

Perhaps you have come through the wilderness and now your testimony is that of the psalmist. In the wilderness you felt as though the "cords of death" entangled you and it was so bad you may have felt "the anguish of the grave" come upon you. Perhaps you were "overcome by trouble and sorrow" (Psalm 116:3, NIV). But now you can declare with the psalmist: "Then I called on the name of the Lord: 'O Lord, save me!' The Lord is gracious and righteous; our God is full of compassion…when I was in great need, he saved me. Be at rest once more, O my soul, for the Lord has been good to you. For you, O Lord, have delivered my soul from death, my eyes from tears, my feet from stumbling" (vv.4-8).

How wonderful it feels to come out of the wilderness and be able to testify to God's mercy and deliverance. He is always faithful to bring us through if we call upon Him.

PRAYER: Thank You, Lord God, for bringing me through the wilderness. Help me to always remember You are a merciful and gracious Deliverer and to call on You as long as I live.

Related verses: Psalm 18:19, 22:4-5, 34:4, 86:13, 107:6

THINK ON THESE THINGS

"… *F*ix your thoughts on what is true and good and right. Think about things that are pure and lovely, and dwell on the fine, good things in others. Think about all you can praise God for and be glad about." Philippians 4:8 (TLB)

How good it is to be out of the wilderness. But the aspects of our situation that "bug us" (the things we can't control) keep trying to catch us off guard and pull us down.

It may seem that many things are wrong in our situation and we can see no way they'll be changed. Those thoughts that cause anxiety lurk just around the corner. We're learning we can't let our minds dwell on these things but instead, we have to give them to God as soon as we *begin* to feel heaviness of spirit—like Peter when he was beginning to sink and cried out to the Lord (Matthew 14:30). Our *beginning* to have that sinking feeling signals the time to cry out to God for help. We have to do as Paul advises in Philippians 4:8 and fix our minds on the fine, good things in others and to think about all we can praise God for and be glad about. The other people in our situation no doubt have some fine and good qualities we can think about and praise God for. No matter how hard our situation, there are blessings too, if we look for them.

PRAYER: Lord God, I give You those thoughts that are trying to drag me down. Help me to see the good in others and in my own situation, and to think on the true and right and lovely.

Related verses: Psalm 94:19; Proverbs 16:3; Isaiah 26:3; Philippians 4:6-7 (TLB)

Made in the USA
Lexington, KY
04 April 2017